Empowering Stories to Activate the Divine Feminine Within

turning point

volume 1

Featured Authors

Windy Cook, Lindsay Marten Ellis, Kathy Forest, Lara O'Neil & Cydya Smith

Plus Essays from 11 Feminine Leaders • Compiled by Astara Jane Ashley

Dearest Patti,
Thank you for accompanying me on this
journey, and for showing me the way
to Li... with an open heart.

FLOWER *of* LIFE PRESS

my love to you

Kristin

Praise

"Having followed Dr. Ericha Scott's writing and enjoyed the privilege of collaborating with her in clinical practice, I can wholeheartedly attest to her penetrating ability to inspire her readers and her clients to dig deep and let their truth shine unabashedly. Dr. Scott wields a sharp intellect with the power to pierce through the haze, combined with an artistry and softness that brings out the mystical. It is her love and passion that I believe gives her the courage to see the self in all it's light and shadow and to help others aspire to their highest selves. In this current work, one cannot come away without feeling truly touched and opened."

—Robert Krochmal, MD, Integrative Wellness

"Kristian's story is rich with vulnerability, humor and heart, as well as the direct and clear transmission of the Divine Mystery. Whether you relate to the courage, healing, and transformation of her journey, or are quickened by Spirit speaking so directly in ways that sets one on their path of heart, you will be inspired! Kristian is a lighthouse of love and sacred spirituality. All she touches is made more alive, liberated, and whole."

—Gabriela Masala, Facilitator, Transformational Guide, Author of
Everyday Magnificent: Practices to Activate an Unlimited Life

"'HELL NO' is a compelling and inspired call to arms for creating sustainable leadership through intention and example. Lara O'Neil's professional journey is powerfully described and poignantly illustrated by intimate personal anecdotes that reveal who she is, what matters to her, and why. While clearly and deeply her own story, it can't help but touch the heart of everyone seeking to be true to themselves. It is the grail quest of every person who has made the sometimes terrifying yet soulfully necessary transition from a life of role and persona to one of authenticity and aliveness. As a focal point, Lara explains the value of combining evidence-based medical science with experience-based alternative medical practices. But this is as much metaphor as it is explanation, as it is not hard to see that the real theme of the chapter is about the power of a wholistic approach—in healing, self-exploration, and self-understanding. Her 'protocol' is a manifesto for self-responsible, integrated living. Ms. O'Neil's message reads like an invitation to the heart of leadership: To guide others to what is possible for them, one must lead from their own personal calling and higher purpose. She lives this."

—George Herrick, Shadow Coach, Artist, Author of *Stone Warrior:
*Confronting Life's Dark Challenges with Stone Art and Meditation***

"Marial is a special and profound person. It is my privilege to have known her for two decades. I am so happy she is bringing her experiences of psychic and goddess healing realms into her writing, and getting the stories published. Everyone in the healing arts should read her work to learn more about open channels, visions that lead to love, energy systems of the aura surrounding our bodies, and that suffering can open into powerful gifts. Everyone in North America should read her work to learn about La Llorona and Tonantzin-Guadalupe, indigenous deities of a continent badly in need of the sacred feminine. And to calm down on panicky days, listen to her music."

—Judy Grahn, PhD, Poet, Cultural Theorist, Author of *The Queen of Swords* and *Blood, Bread, and Roses: How Menstruation Created the World*

"Kristin Ford is as gifted with language and storytelling as she is with bridging the gap between this physical, tangible world and the infinitely more subtle spiritual realms. This piece is at once heart-wrenching and inspiring. In vulnerably sharing her journey through a childhood shaped by the particulars of her own family system, combined with broader cultural forces familiar to many of us, Kristin reveals her innocent and highly-relatable choice to belong at the expense of honoring her true Self. This is a recounting of her journey home—towards reclaiming those aspects of herself that were actively hidden for so long. Kristin's story illustrates the power each of us has to choose to be fully who we are, in our 'unique radiance,' as she puts it. We would all do well to follow in her footsteps."

—Melody Mischke, Co-Founder of Truth Love + Marketing®

"Lindsay's sacred journey invites you to discover what's possible for you when you invite your pain to guide you, allowing yourself to feel to the depths of your being and melt the armor around your heart. It's in the moments where we choose to courageously explore our hearts that we get to experience the expansiveness of witnessing the miraculous in the mundane, connecting to the Divine within us and embodying our wholeness. This book is an empowering invitation of deep remembrance and a coming home to ourselves, where we trust our inner knowing and feel alive in our bodies to experience the fullness of life and love."

—Yvette Duncan, Founder of Pearls of Luminous Love

"Crystal's radical self-awareness based on reality and compassion serves as a guide-in-action of how we too can be more self-aware with kindness towards ourselves and others. This is accomplished by purely living in the now and experiencing what each moment has to offer, even in moments of crisis. This written word weaves art, nature, family, and forgiveness into every word. It inspires. Digging deep into tough topics of our lives can show us the path to acceptance and for-giveness—this is my main takeaway. While it may seem simplistic, Crystal tackles a set of tough topics with the grace and clarity to make it simply stated. It is a mes-sage that is deeply personal yet accessible and relatable. What a world we would live in if we all aspired to be this radical."

—Rosie Hartmann, Author of *Arise, Go Forth and Conquer*

"I was deeply moved by Jennifer Belanger's story in *Turning Point: Empowering Stories to Activate the Divine Feminine Within.* Jennifer has a rare gift and profound ability to connect and relay synchronicities, timelines, signs, and symbols related to her amazing path and experiences. I can see that she is helping align people to the pathway of their own unique story; their sacred treasures of inner wisdom, greater awareness, and a deep connection to God. I simply LOVE the title, 'Archaeology of My Soul' as over time, it has come together like a symphony of music—her incred-ible insights, mystical experiences, visions, and what her work is doing for others. Jennifer marries her writing with sacred breathwork, as she assists people to access their own archives, their own archaeological site within of their soul's story. When her next book, *Archaeology of My Soul* comes out, I cannot wait to read it!"

—Deborra Cameron, Emotional Blueprint Coach

"The first thought that came into my mind upon reading Judith's life review was what a braveness and divine victory it is to express and reveal such sincere and honest heart, pouring openly out the secrets of her bitter-sweet alchemical trans-formative journey of turning ocean-deep wounds into understanding, inner truth and wisdom; that is how freedom is born from the Soul. The 'final dance with her beloved cat upon her death' was so moving that touched our own similar heartbreaking moments of saying farewells... Judith's story is a beautiful example of dancing through the shadowland to reach the Light that cannot be taken away because it shines from the inside out..."

—Dr. Beatrix Czeizel, Author of the *Stellar Nations–Soul Families,*
Stellar Destinies, and *Calling You*

"Our raison d'être is a question we all ask, yet one whose answer few consciously seek. Cydya Smith is one of the rare true seekers. What a strange and wonderful convergence of forces we see in her story: a deeply connected family embracing her with all their heart, and she, the seeker, throwing her arms open to embrace the world with all her soul. We feel the dismay of the nine-year-old learning that death comes to us all, the rebellion of the teenager who feels the pull of her own talents and desires against the push-back of family who only want her to be safe and successful. We feel, though we may never have experienced, the physical sensations she felt, of spirits, presences, forces—whatever you would like to call them—from the other side. We recognize and marvel at the sense of wonder that floods us as serendipitous discoveries tumble into our lives the more we seek, the more we see, the more we listen to the voices within. Cydya's is a beautiful story, distilled at the end into a gorgeous soul-birthed poem."

—Ann Voorhees Baker, Founder of Women At Woodstock

"In an inspiring story of 'startling transformation,' Christina Mercy shares profound experiences of death and rebirth in vivid imagery leading us to the heart of the fire. Offering us a glimpse of the powerful inner and outer Phoenix, Mercy helps us understand that everything happens to open our hearts. Canvas and paints provided a canvas portal into the depths of her female-incarnated experience. With archetypal language and imagery, she presents a stunning love story to the self, describing personal soul retrieval with lush words and paintings. Mercy offers stunning glimpses of her mission—through spiritual alchemy—to reach the truth that can begin to heal our ancestral patterns."

—Susan Wooldridge, Author of *Poemcrazy: Freeing Your Life with Words*

"Kirsty pulls back the veil to allow us to see the truth of grief and past the life buoy of gratitude we all so often cling to, instead shining the light on the depths of complex emotion that feel as if they could drown us. By sharing her story and being so vulnerable, she shows us that we're not alone—that wherever we are in the grief journey, we can emerge to a new truth and knowing, gilded by it and not broken. Her writing is a joy and blessing, and I know it will bring comfort to so many."

—Felicity Wingrove

"Thank you, Windy, for sharing your powerful, breathtakingly honest insights of surviving. For showing that surviving is possible, even if at times it may feel impossible. You survived: physically, mentally and emotionally—yes, deeply hurt—with cracks all over your heart and soul. Gently recovering, allowing cracks to become scars, with much stronger tissues. Like Kintsugi, the Japanese Art of repairing broken porcelain with Gold, these pieces become more precious after the crash. Windy, you and your beautiful family, as well as every soul reading this: May you heal your cracks/wounds and shine your enforced version of yourself through gold."

—**Sinja Woltemath**

"Sitting down to read Caryl's turning-point story was a personal joy. Caryl is a natural storyteller. Telling her story in a witty, engaging, wry, laugh-out-loud relatable way, I want to know more about her truths and her wisdom. Caryl leans in and narrates her turning-point story to you from a place where you know she's now safe and happy. As a reader, you will go anywhere to listen to her; go anywhere for her. Her upcoming memoir will touch and heal many broken hearts. I am listening…"

—**Alvagh Cronin, Author of** *The Bridge of Now*

"Kathy Forest's chapter 'Becoming a Radical Revolutionary' was a heart opening to compassion for my long journey to find my contribution as a divine feminine conduit for Source. Kathy's mission to share how women can fully access their power through their bodies is so needed. Her journey and her teachings are essential to women's empowerment so they can become the leaders that are needed now."

—**Judy Keating, M.A., Co-author of**
F.A.I.T.H. Finding answers in the Heart, vol. 2

"It is the first woman who dances in a circle of fire that makes it safe enough for the rest of us to let go and become whole again. In *Turning Point,* Katie Fink bravely holds her heart out to us and shares a rocky awakening for all to see; a divinely timed lesson for females of all kinds. There is a rawness in the beauty as she unpacks what some would consider insurmountable life changes. She breaks taboos and opens the curtain on ways women in crisis can support each other and, in turn, themselves. As a health optimization coach, I know that the body, mind, and spirit are carefully woven into every choice we make. And yet, I often see women second guess pivotal moments of clarity that could help them shift into their best wellness, careers, or romances. This book recognizes, and empowers us through an understanding that we are equally sensitive as we are powerful—a reminder to awaken both sides of our divine feminine—where our greatest capacity lies. Consider reading this book as full permission granted, to tap into your intuitive gifts, sister, release what holds you back; and call in every last one of your weirdest, wildest and greatest dreams."

—Kristin Weitzel, Founder: Warrior Woman Mode/SHERPA Breath & Cold, Host of WELLPOWER

FLOWER *of* LIFE PRESS

Flower of Life Press
Hadlyme, CT.

To contact the publisher, visit www.floweroflifepress.com

Book cover and interior design by Astara Jane Ashley, www.floweroflifepress.com
Cover art by Christina Mercy, www.paintsinstardust.com

Library of Congress Control Number: Available Upon Request

ISBN-13: 979-8-9873954-0-0

Printed in the United States of America

Dedication

This book is dedicated to all the Sacred Feminine Voices that have been oppressed and suppressed for eons...

May they be heard, received and honored Always and in All Ways.

To our ancestors who have gone before, we are grateful to you as our way-showers and for your courage in leading the way.

Contents

featured authors

contributing authors

Saving My Heart

By Christina Mercy, LCSW CHt RYT200

Encrypted with codes, symbols and light language, this paintings' message to me is, "I've got you, and I'm keeping your heart safe until you can heal." I hadn't realized she was keeping my heart safe until much later. Mysteriously and intuitively, many of my archetypal paintings held pieces of my heart. This was the first painting I created weeks after losing my home to the huge Paradise fire; which incidentally was accompanied by a series of massive initiations which lasted for a few years. The Phoenix was instinctually guided to extinguish various parts of Northern California, and other locations of the world. I have said, "My home, art work, and marriage were sacrificed to the Phoenix." Little did I know what a powerful Turning Point the Phoenix would introduce to my soul.

SAVING MY HEART

Emerging before dawn,
Past pine trees and mighty Oaks...
Woodpeckers made their homes in hollow wooden holes.
Blue Jays built their nests, and shared the sky with hawks and common crows.
It was nearly winter; The Solstice weeks ahead.
The fierce winds blew through the canyon,
Roaring its bellows, while shifting everything...
You could hear The Phoenix screeching, as she fanned her commanding wings.
Skunks, racoons and foxes looked up, as the land began to look very strange,
In one cataclysmic instance, their entire life had changed.
It is true she is a legend; some say she is a myth.
She was on an instinctual mission, setting everything a blaze,
Her intuition guiding her to leave one immortal egg.
I have been initiated by the Phoenix...
And friends will say the same.
The fire took my lover, as I watched my life go up in flames.
The Phoenix had a purpose, to burn the past away...
I had to save my own heart; I would never be the same.
Fragments scattered far and near, I had to call these soul parts home.
The Phoenix sheltered me in darkness, leaving tears to heal my weary bones.
Her spirit whispers through the cosmos, "light will be coming soon. Stay strong, chose love, in the cycles of the Moon."
Emerging before dawn, past pine trees and mighty oaks, woodpeckers made their homes in hollow wooden holes.

Introduction

By Astara Jane Ashley, M.A.

Publisher, Flower of Life Press

"My purpose is to share 1 million women's voices with the world."

When I heard the words come out of my mouth, I almost fell over.

1 million? It's impossible! Who do you think you are? How could that EVER happen? Are you crazy? Go get a REAL job!

The old familiar voices of self-doubt instantly crept in—until I took a breath, grounded and calmed myself, and remembered an important saying that has served me well over the years:

"Without risk, there is no truth."

This was something I had heard years ago from an energy healer that I was seeing with my then-boyfriend. I had been doubting my relationship and was feeling unsure about taking the next steps into marriage. But after months of working with this healer and letting go of all of the stress around family and societal expectations, I had a vision of my future daughters... and the words *family* and *commitment* came into my mind's eye. I knew in that moment I needed to take the risk—no matter how scared I was of getting divorced. These souls were waiting for me to bring them in, and this was the person for me to partner with.

Ultimately, I did face a huge turning point by leaving my marriage after ten years and getting divorced, which marked the beginning of my journey of learning how to love and accept myself, release old shame and destructive patterns, open my heart, and claim my birthright as an embodied sovereign feminine being—and mother—on this planet.

Since that turning point, I have vowed to be an emissary of the Divine and to walk the path of the Priestess, a path that is in service to community and asks me to ripple out the vibration of LOVE from my essential core. It's a path that allows me to say *yes* to love and *no* to fear and control.

There are many painful turning points that humans face—divorce, hatred, war, violence, death, illness, separation, etc. Divorce was just one turning point that woke me up and propelled me forward into my own conscious evolution. But since that time in 2009, there have been many more, and I know there will be plenty more in the years ahead.

When life's initiations happen, usually the old voices of doubt seep back in. In fact, recently, my puppy and I were attacked by a rottweiler and I had my ear bitten and torn, requiring stitches. My pup had two surgeries to repair her wounds. It was unexpected and terrifying. And yet, I still have complete trust and faith that life is FOR me—not against me. The trauma has cleared fairly quickly. Now, I can see the gift on the other side of pain; I can see the healing that is available to all of us through the power of our words; I can *feel* the joy, authenticity, and integrity of showing up in my truth and standing tall like a tree—rooted yet flexible.

So where did we, as women, learn to suppress the painful and grief-filled parts of ourselves? And how do we get through life's turning points and dark nights of the soul back into the light of new beginnings and an open heart?

- We face the fear of being vulnerable and allow ourselves to feel our feelings.
- We tell the truth and strive for an honest and authentic life.
- We release the masks of who we *think* we are supposed to be and show up as we truly are by calling home all the parts of ourselves we've disowned.
- We open our minds and our hearts to embrace forgiveness.
- We cultivate confidence and commitment to keep our vibration high and keep our heads above water.
- We release people-pleasing and *risk it all for truth,* no matter what people say, or who gets triggered.
- We are *willing* to be projected upon by others while holding exceptional boundaries and compassion, all in the service of LOVE.

All of this requires courage, commitment, and a willingness to embody our fierce and primal instincts. It's messy, that's for sure! And SO beautifully painful. However, a broken heart mends and can then *transmit* the power that love offers.

Inside of these pages are the stories of 16 women—their roles as Priestesses, artists, healers, medicine women, your neighbor next door, and mothers may vary, but they are all daughters of the Divine and doing the work of cultivating LOVE. They are willing to risk judgment in order to speak their sovereign truth—no matter what. They know that our transformation as individuals, communities, and a global village is of the utmost importance, and are raw and real as they vulnerably share the stories that have carried them from voiceless to empowered.

Each story in this book matters, and so dear reader, does YOURS. The journey is challenging and takes on urgency in these fractious times, and so I invite you to ponder these questions as you read ahead:

What in your life are you willing to release so that you may fully step into your power to use YOUR voice and message for positive change on the planet?

Where are you resisting facing your own life's turning points and seeing the gifts in the experience? Are you willing to take a peek and do it anyways, regardless of your fear, knowing you are NOT alone?

You can read this book from front to back or choose to open the book at random as use it as an oracle and a guiding light in that moment. My wish for you is that you will recognize yourself in one aspect of one story—no matter how small. This book offers you permission to seek your own truth—because the possibilities for your potential and for an amazing, gratitude-filled life are infinite!

In the meantime, I will continue onward to share 1 million women's voices via their stories. I look forward to being in community with you, and sharing Volume 2 of this Turning Point series in the summer of 2023.

With love,
Astara

Featured Author

CHAPTER 1

Everything But The Kitchen Sink

How a Firestorm Ignited My Heart

By Windy Gordon Cook

When was the last time you sunk your teeth into an "Everything But the Kitchen Sink" cookie?

Did you like it?

If you did, was it because in every bite there is something different?

A rich chocolate chip, a toffee cluster, a raisin, a salty pretzel, or the crunchy surprise of sea salt?

I've heard people describe an "everything but the kitchen sink" cookie as the cookie that has it all.

Literally, the entire kitchen pantry is in that cookie.

My tennis coach, Stacie Bowman hinted that is what I should bring to my tennis game: "Everything but the kitchen sink."

"What does that mean exactly?" I asked her.

"If you can bring as much variety of your shots to the court, it keeps your opponent guessing, you will have the advantage and you will increase your chances of winning."

In the world of tennis, a variety of shots would include a slice, inside-out forehand, overhead, lob, drop shot, volley, and backhand. Stacie has an entire tennis drill called, "Everything But The Kitchen Sink."

Variety is what makes life interesting.

Isn't it what we all crave?

I meet Stacie, who is brilliant and one of the best coaches I've ever had, once a week in Louisville on the Davidson Mesa. It's a stand-alone tennis court with beautiful views of the Flatirons and Spanish Hills in the distance.

Every week it gets a little *easier* to look out on the mesa.

It was on the Davidson mesa where our house once stood.

My daughter and I left that morning. We never returned.

It was 10:30 a.m. December 30th, 2021. It was winter.

The sky looked unusual that morning.

The wind was something fierce as if it had a life all its own, not your typical December day.

It was unseasonably warm and dry and the windows of our house shook from high gusts of 100 mph winds.

We got in the car, buckled our seat belts, and drove down the driveway.

My daughter pointed west, in the direction of the mountains.

The flatirons, jutting up to the sky, a rock-solid presence seemed to point to wafering smoke in the distance.

We both couldn't help but notice the yellow hazy air. I wonder if there is a brush fire? I thought to myself.

Brush fires are common.

Our fire department is only a few minutes away…

We drove south heading to Denver, the sky was blue and strangely serene. I tried to forget the last week and the long days over the holidays that our teenage daughter, Aubrielle had been in her room.

I tried to forget hearing her cry and the loneliness she felt confined to her room. She had contracted the Covid-19 virus after performing in a candlelight choir performance with her school.

Covid was not our friend and it stole everything that mattered to us.

We had given up seeing our family, traveling to places, eating at our favorite restaurants, and seeing the beautiful smiles on our friends' faces.

Covid was killing people. Hospitals all over the country were full.

Full of people who could no longer breathe.

In December 2021, the Marshall Fire killed two people and destroyed 1,084 homes in Louisville, Superior, and unincorporated Boulder County.

It is considered the most destructive wildfire in Colorado's history.

Theories on the cause of the fire have ranged from downed utility lines to a continuously burning underground coal seam fire to a religious sect whose members sometimes burn trash on the property.

"The cause of the blaze is still undetermined."
—The Denver Post

Cherry Creek Mall was bright and shiny with holiday decorations and swarms of people returning Christmas gifts.

My daughter and I decided to briefly split up. I was going to return a nightgown and she was going to use a gift card.

We made a plan to meet up and shop together for the afternoon. I walked out of the store to see Aubrielle running toward me.

"Dad is trying to call you!"

"What?"

"There's a huge fire on the mesa. People are evacuating."

"What?" People are evacuating?

I couldn't believe what I was hearing.

I looked down at my phone and my ringer was turned off.

Off…

I looked and there were several missed calls from my husband. I had a sudden terrible feeling in my stomach that he had not been able to reach me.

I dialed his number quickly.

"Chris?" I said in a quick voice. " What's going on?"

"The town of Superior is evacuating. Smoke is encircling the house. We've got to leave. We've got to leave now!"

Smoke from a rapidly approaching firestorm encircled our home on the Mesa and it quickly became hard for homeowners to see.

As the reality hit my husband, he calmly asked our twins to put a few of their things in thier carry-on suitcases.

The twins began to cry as they packed up their favorite stuffed animals, blankies, and other beloved things.

Chris walked into our home office, grabbed the computers, our passports, birth certificates, immunization cards, leashed the dog, and got everyone in the car.

At the last minute, my husband remembered to grab my tennis racquet. Of all the things, he grabbed one of my most precious belongings.

Tennis is my passion, my sanctuary, my therapy, and my rock. It allows me to get completely in the moment, be present and forget everything.

We had never talked about a situation like what we would do in a wildfire.

Our neighbors to the north and south of us were leaving in a panic, the smoke thick with debris made it difficult to see the road.

Chris decided to drive up over the median and head north away from the congested traffic.

Hundreds of cars were all trying to do the same thing. Escape the fire.

Aubrielle and I ran to the car. "Where should we go?"

"We can't go home," I told her.

I took a deep breath and I called my brother, Ben.

Hello?" Ben answered.

"Windy?"

"Yes," I said

"You should drive to Mom's place in Denver and wait there. I saw on the national news there's a terrible fire in Louisville."

"Mom and Danny are in Florida. How are we going to get in?

"Her neighbor has a key. You should wait there," he said.

I turned to look at Aubrielle and she nodded in agreement.

"Let's go."

"Okay," she answered back.

We drove to my Mother's condominium and walked up to the neighbor's door. The neighbor opened the door before we knocked and handed us the key.

I could hear the news in the background. They knew about the fire.

We walked inside and sat down.

We turned on the news and watched in horror.

Our entire neighborhood was on fire. The "Davidson Mesa" sign which stood at the path leading to our house was in plain view, the reporter was standing by the smoke, and flames were all around in close proximity.

"If you live on the mesa, your home may be on fire."

I couldn't believe what I was seeing.

It was something out of an apocalyptic horror movie.

I heard the door open and in walked Chris, my husband, our ten-year-old twins, and our dog.

We hugged hard, looked at each other, and without saying anything, we watched the T.V. for hours.

Scenes began to unfold and the impossible happened.

The fire raged on, firefighters were fighting not only the flames but winds of up to 100 miles per hour.

A *firestorm* is what they called it.

A *firestorm*.

I had never heard the term before.

We found out later, that the firefighters were fighting a losing battle of the relentless wind and had to pick and choose between homes that were already a "lost cause" and homes that maybe had a chance to be saved.

What a gut-wrenching decision to make. My friend Crystal's husband is a firefighter. I can't imagine what fighting that fire was like for him.

The firestorm was unstoppable, consuming everything in its path, and never seemed to cease.

We watched the news until we couldn't watch anymore. We went to sleep that night. Two of us on the bed, two of us on the pull-out couch, and one on the floor.

That night I lay awake tossing and turning, unsure if we would wake to our house still standing or just ashes.

It was December 31st, 2021.

That morning I awoke with a headache and a horrible feeling of dread. We received a text message from our neighbor along with a picture of what looked to be our backyard.

We had trouble identifying where the picture was taken but I could make out the stone pillars of our back gate and backyard.

"I'm so sorry...the message read." This is what is left of your backyard, your home and our neighborhood.

Ashes and rubble were all that was left of our home.

I read the text message again, not believing it. Our house couldn't have been burned down. It was stucco, with a concrete roof and stone tiles.

"Oh no," I said to my husband and I felt as if the wind had been knocked out of me and I buckled over.

I felt sick and unable to move.

Our children started to cry and I reached for my husband. We just held each other for what felt like hours, not knowing what to do next.

We had just lost everything: everything but the clothes on our backs.

Everything but the kitchen sink.

Our nightmare was our reality.

We called our family and no one could believe what had just happened.

What were we going to do? Where were we going to go?

We were now homeless. We were now a homeless family of five and a dog.

I have family that lives in the New Orleans area. They survived Hurricane Katrina.

Water, not fire, was their enemy and flooding destroyed their home and life as they knew it. I thought about how we weren't the only ones who have lost everything to a natural disaster. We weren't alone.

I think my Aunt Jackie said it took years to recuperate, rebuild, and regroup after the hurricane.

I just didn't think something like this would happen to us.

My mind was flooded, and foggy, and I couldn't stand up. I couldn't think and I lost track of time. I choked back the tears and couldn't move.

I called my Mother and she was in total shock. She tried to get on the next plane back home but it was the holiday season and flights were booked. She was hundreds of miles away with a shared heartache.

Questions loomed.

Where had the fire come from?

We turned on the news and reporters were confirming the worst.

Our entire neighborhood was gone.

The firestorm consumed the entire Davidson Mesa, Harper Lake, parts of Superior, Spanish Hills, and Coal Creek. The list grew…

I looked out the windows and wondered, "Where was the snow? Isn't it winter?"

We wanted to drive back to see what was left of our home but police and firefighters urged people to stay out of the area since it was unsafe and fires were still raging on.

I had my own conversation going on in my mind. *Where is the cold snow that blankets the mesa this time of year?*

How could a fire jump a highway?

My cell phone rang and it was my Aunt Angela. I was grateful to hear her calm, caring voice. She's a doctor and she's seen PTSD in "real-time" and knew what to do.

"Honey, I'm so sorry. I can't believe you just lost your home. Get a paper and a pen and write down these things," Angela told me.

First: Drink Water

Second: Eat food

Third: Sleep

Fourth: Clothing—pajamas for the kids, underwear, a coat, and boots.

The list was simple but I couldn't think straight and I couldn't write.

"I love you," she said, "You are all so lucky to be alive. It's all going to be okay."

And so I did. I packed everyone up in the car and we headed to get pajamas, underwear, a coat, and some boots.

As we drove home, it started to snow and I stared up at the sky wondering why it couldn't have snowed 24 hours ago.

It felt like a cruel joke Mother Nature had played on us.

I was angry and sad.

I felt devastated in every cell of my body.

"How is this happening?" I asked myself over and over again.

I was numb and wondering when I would wake up.

It was New Year's Eve and people were leaving in their party best, with horns, hats, and bottles of champagne.

I wished we had something to celebrate.

Our nightmare had just started.

Chris started calling hotels in the area. We immediately thought of the Marriott Residence Inn because they generally have a kitchen, complimentary breakfast, and laundry facilities.

We didn't know how long we would be staying there, but one thing we did know, we didn't have a home to go back to and it was the middle of winter.

Chris called quite a few Marriotts but I would hear him say each time. "Okay, I understand. Thank you." Hundreds of families were now homeless and people were filling up every hotel and motel in the area.

After several failed attempts, Chris finally talked to the manager of the Boulder Marriott who made a room available to us and we headed there that evening.

We packed up the kids and the dog and drove to Boulder. We stayed there for almost a month.

It was so cold. The snow came and never left. I cursed it, but it became a constant companion, something to count on and it greeted us each day.

And so did the people.

People began to bring over food.

A lot of food.

Tara, our daughter's Waldorf high school started a meal train.

It was amazing.

One of our favorite dinners was brought over by our friends Casey and Scott.

They made homemade lasagna, and a salad and it tasted like home. It was the first homemade meal we had since the fire. Our dear friend, Melanie also brought over a white lasagna and it was divine.

Her card read, "To love someone is to feed them."

That's how it felt.

We ate love.

Every night we digested love in all savory flavors.

There was a knock on the door and it was our dear friend Jill. She walked in with a big bouquet of flowers, a basket full of food, and essentials. She was a breath of fresh air and she stayed for hours sharing updates on the fire. She gave us a book titled, *A Fire Story* by Brian Fies.

A Fire Story is a firsthand account of the author, Brian's experience of the devastating California wildfires that destroyed his home and left many of his neighbors' families broken and homeless.

That book was a helpful resource and gave us a "road map" to our tragedy. Wildfires in California are common. People lose their homes every fire season and rebuild and move on. Maybe that is why my cousins Kate and Elizabeth were one of the first of our family members to put together care packages packed full of sweatshirts and tennis clothes from California.

We had so many care packages and people who then stopped by.

People brought homemade meals, games, clothes, and hugs. People also prayed for us. There is an undeniable power of prayer and I am a huge believer of that collective power. It was as if God was holding us in both palms.

The entire community of the Ranch gave us gift cards, clothes, money, and hope.

My Aunt Patti sent a beautiful Lemurian crystal that I would hold at night to keep calm and to bring me peace.

Every morning my soul sister, Sinja who lives in Germany would message me an "Angel of the day" to inspire me and keep me going. The first image was always blurry because my eyes would pool with tears. My favorite angel message she sent me was of a beautiful angel radiating light with the word "Empfangen" or to receive the angelic blessing. It was powerful and I could feel the light emanating from the phone.

I felt rich in love. We were rich with spiritual abundance and it just kept growing.

Mackintosh, our twins' school, gave us school supplies, handmade bookshelves, books, free lunches, and warm clothing to help us get by.

We ate dinner together in the cramped little hotel room, oftentimes not talking but just eating, too tired for conversation.

Our good friends Karli and Kaj headed the call and started a Go-Fund-Me page on Facebook. People were calling nonstop asking us what they could do to help us and a Go-Fund-Me site provided a place to start. Karli is a force, and an angel. She grew up in a military family and she fought for us just like a soldier would. Karli visited donation sites and brought warm jackets and outdoor gear back to us.

Donations began to pour in. So many of our friends and family donated to our GoFundMe page and it was so appreciated. When we would go out in public, people would ask us what we needed.

We didn't know what to say. We didn't know what we needed.

We needed everything.

Where should we start?

That morning I woke up and felt so overwhelmed I didn't know where to begin. I looked for our dog and his leash and walked outside.

The ground was covered in snow and I felt the familiar pain in my chest.

Nausea was a feeling I felt all of the time. I lost my appetite but Jenny our friend brought a ninja food mixer so I could drink protein-rich smoothies. She knows I love them.

The days were spent making lists of things to do and endless talks with our insurance agent.

The sun came and left and the days melted away.

I felt discombobulated, unrooted, and uncertain. Insomnia was my middle name. Maybe that was the way it was meant to be. I was awake to comfort my kids when they would wake with nightmares.

Our time was spent doing exactly what was on my Aunt's list. We drank water, ate food, slept, and stayed warm.

The hardest part was that we couldn't go home. Our neighborhood was blocked off and the only thing we could do was watch the news and get updates on the recovery. It's human nature not to believe something unless you can see it with your own eyes.

We watched the news but it wasn't the same. The Marshall Fire was making national headlines.

President Biden flew out to our neighborhood on the presidential plane and declared the Marshall Fire a national emergency and FEMA got involved.

It was something to see our very own President visit our little neighborhood of Louisville.

On the news that day, we learned that victims of the Marshall Fire could register with FEMA and be eligible for services, receive Red Cross money, and find out about programs to help fire victims.

Our world was shattered but slowly the community was coming together. Ascent Church provided support and my dear friend Cindy gave us two checks from her ministry practice and a beautiful bible. A small group of Baptist volunteers offered to help us sift through the burned rubble of our lot in an attempt to find any of our possessions. We found nothing except our stainless steel sink.

Jewish Family Services offered PTSD treatments, bilateral music, and acupuncture.

About a hundred of us survivors gathered at the local recreation center in Louisville that weekend to partake in bilateral sound therapy.

We sat at tables and downloaded music on Spotify. Men, women, and children listened to the bilateral music with headphones.

I closed my eyes and the music took me through the entire fire experience all over again, playing out like a movie. Somehow my brain was processing the trauma and providing resolution.

I slept better that night.

I learned from a volunteer that bi-lateral music, a form of EMDR or otherwise known as eye movement desensitization and reprocessing therapy is becoming a popular, simple, and cost-effective treatment for victims of PTSD. This treatment is being widely used now for victims of natural disasters, first responders, survivors of mass shootings, and war veterans.

Bilateral sounds, alternating between the left and right ears through headphones create a "calm parallel to the activation of trauma." After just one session, people report feeling more relaxed and less activated by the memories of trauma.

I opened the local news and learned about several donation events.

We got motivated to go to the Rayback Collective in Boulder which was an enormous clothing and home goods donation event.

We walked into a huge indoor beer garden where we were met with tons of volunteers.

It was surreal to find ourselves there. In the past, I have been a philanthropist, giving money and clothes away but now we were on the receiving end.

There were piles and piles of clothes, shoes, and household goods.

Quite honestly, we didn't know where to begin.

I choked back the tears and I was overcome with emotion. The reality kept hitting me over and over.

We lost everything in the fire.

I gathered my emotions. Dried the tears off and looked at so many faces of my neighbors who were also looking for clothes. It felt like a bad dream. A really bad dream.

"Windy," I heard my name being called as I looked up to see my dear old friend Casey. She had a smile on her face and she hugged me with her entire body.

"I'll help you," she said. "What size are you?"

Casey helped me that day. More than she will ever know. She helped me walk tall and find warm clothes; helped me to focus and not get overwhelmed.

I sometimes would wander around in the warehouse and get lost. Lost in my thoughts and just lost...I was looking through the eyes of post-traumatic stress disorder.

I was overwhelmed and shaking all over.

I would pick up the clothes and then put them down. I was looking for my things.

It was strange. Jill also kept me sane by looking for items for our twins and carrying donations to the car.

At one point, I found myself rummaging through baby items. "Windy... you don't have a baby," I heard a voice whisper.

After the third day of going to the Rayback, I realized I wasn't even looking for things anymore. I was looking for a safe place to cry.

"Are you okay?" a volunteer asked me. She reached out her hand and I took it, and then I sat down and cried.

I cried and I cried.

I cried deep sobs of grief and sobs of tremendous loss.

The enormity of losing our beloved home and life as we knew it was immense—like an ocean—and there didn't seem to be an end to my sadness and grief.

I walked outside of the Rayback Collective to sit by the fire pit and the food trucks. A friendly face met me there. It was Melissa, a dear friend that I played tennis with. "Here's a care package, lady!"

She drove up the alley, rolled the windows, and handed me a lovely bag of pajamas, wine, and other goodies.

"This is from Pam and me," she said. "We love you and it's going to be okay."

I hugged her and I was so glad to get warm pajamas.

After that day, I didn't go back to the Rayback Collective.

It felt like our world was torn apart but I had finally let go of some of the sadness. I felt like I was ready to turn the page.

I was writing a new chapter. "How to begin again."

Little by little, we began to replace our clothing but we didn't have any household goods.

It was overwhelming to think about all that we needed.

This is where my mother stepped in. There's no one who knows what you need for a kitchen like your mother. She organized a "kitchen shower" with all of her best girlfriends.

"Everything in a junk drawer" was the theme and it was just that, except junk isn't the term I would use. When you don't have anything junk becomes a necessity.

God bless Joan for hosting that shower! Ladies brought their smiles, their kitchen essentials, their stories, and junk drawer items.

We sat in Joan's living room and we shared tears.

Think about your kitchen for a minute and all that it holds... Yes, pots, pans, glasses, and dishes but does it also hold the laughter and best memories of life shared with family and friends?

My kitchen was my favorite place in my home. It was "my heartbeat" and always the place everyone would gather.

It was at that very gathering in Joan's living room where my broken heart felt like beating again. Throughout time and space, the sacred circle of women coming together in times of need is precious. I am so grateful for the women in my life and for one particular man: My husband, Chris. He was everything I wasn't.

He was calm, collected, and razor-focused. He got a notebook at a grocery store and made the calls you are supposed to make when you lose your home to a fire.

He called our insurance agent, our neighbors, and close friends. He learned from a neighbor that there were several Enclave neighbors on our street who were going to hire a private debris removal company to expedite the clearing of our lot.

He called the architect that built our home to get the plans to rebuild our home, hired a public adjuster, and called my mother-in-law and secured temporary housing at her home in north Boulder. Thank goodness for Diane. We were so grateful to have a place to call home temporarily.

After a few conversations, we decided not to rebuild and it was the best decision we have ever made. We looked north, to a new town, a new community, and a chance to leave it all behind.

Leaving it all behind…the loss, the memories of what was, and the sadness.

The Arkansas River carried us forward in the months to follow and we traveled down it with our close friends, Jackie and Jeff.

Thank goodness for that beautiful river and for Jackie and Jeff. They have been like family to us, giving us so much, helping us to laugh again, and to replace our much-needed household items.

We started our trip in Buena Vista. You could only bring a few things on the raft. The river took us for miles, the scenery ever-changing.

I couldn't stop gazing at the ripples in the water, a constant reminder of change, the ebb, and flow of life.

Our raft guide shared with us that the Arkansas River is his favorite river because it is so crystal clear, unlike other rivers that are murky and muddy with sediment. I felt my mind becoming crystal clear just like the river.

Have you ever thought about how a river never goes back to where it starts? It's always moving forward.

Forward.

It was there on that river that I realized what I truly needed.

I need my family, my friends, and my faith, and I need this. I need to be in nature.

That night I had a dream.

I walked up our driveway, the rose bushes met me there...

I reached and opened the front door.

I walked inside our home and the morning sun streamed through the windows.

It was so peaceful. A warm feeling filled every sense of my body.

I walked outside onto our flagstone patio and watched the sunset paint the tall grass with a golden hue of honey, the light of the dying sun.

I heard the laughter of our children and felt my husband holding my hand. I was home. Home where I was safe, rooted, and where I belonged.

Then I awoke from my dream and knew I would never see our home again. It was gone, gone with the firestorm.

If you had just a few minutes to collect your most precious thing, what would you take with you?

What would it be?

The big question I ask myself now is, "Is my pain or my passion going to define me?"

And that is my turning point.

The pain in my heart of losing our home isn't going away anytime soon.

Ultimately most things can be replaced except for one.

My identity.

I feel like the fire took my identity and burned it along with our home and everything we owned. My identity was in my home office. All of the books I wrote and contributed essays for, all of my teaching resources and Instructor manuals, pictures of my students and classes that I taught, my degrees and accolades, and all of the philanthropic work that I had worked hard to accomplish was all gone.

Replacing it is not what I have to do.

Reinventing myself is.

I'm not the same person I was before the fire. I'm rewriting my future. Rewriting my destiny.

I'm brawny, vigilant, tenacious, rugged, more present, and grateful for the little things.

The little things, such as a hug from my children, being able to laugh, drink water, have food, warm clothes, and a safe place to rest my head.

I'm still an author, a teacher, a therapist, a passionate tennis player, and a Thetahealer. I'm still a mother and a wife but I am also more.

I am a survivor with a second chance at life. I survived the Marshall Fire—the most destructive fire in Colorado history.

I see with new eyes that find each moment precious.

When you go through a life-changing experience and escape with your life, you have a new perspective.

Things and possessions take on a new meaning.

You realize what matters most.

I have my children, my beloved partner, my husband, and my dog. So many of our neighbors couldn't rescue their pets.

Loss on the level of irreplaceable.

Life is a gift.

I want to do everything I can, and experience everything I can.

I want to rewrite my life with the questions, "How can I live life to the fullest?" "Who can I help?" and, "How can I serve?" "How can I be someone's angel who needs one."

Now, I look at life with gratitude and wonder.

Time is priceless and non-negotiable.

Every morning I greet the sunrise with gratitude for everyone that helped us.

Everyone.

I remember every little and big thing that someone did for us.

The power of the human spirit is tremendous and awe-inspiring.

Who do I want to be and what do I want to bring to the table?

My answer is, *"Everything but the kitchen sink."*

Special acknowledgment to Diane White—thank you for being our Angel.

WINDY GORDON COOK *is the best-selling author of* The Sisterhood of The Mindful Goddess *and is a contributing author to several books in the best-selling* New Feminine Evolutionary *series:* The New Feminine Evolutionary, Sacred Body Wisdom, Sovereign Onto Herself, Practice, *and* Set Sail. *She is also the author of "Following Windy," an interactive blog for mothers struggling with issues at "Moms Like Me."*

Windy is a graduate of the Journey of Young Women Mentoring Girls Certificate Training and enjoys volunteering at her children's school as the classroom "room parent." She also has formal training as a physio-neuro trainer, is certified in Reiki II, and is a ThetaHealing™ practitioner and instructor. Windy's ThetaHealing classes "Basic DNA," "Manifestation and Abundance" as well as "You & Creator," are favorites of her students.

Windy's path includes work as a family therapist at Denver Children's Home for troubled youth and as a third-grade teacher in an inner-city school for gifted and talented children. She holds a master's degree in Educational Psychology from the University of Colorado at Denver and a master's degree in social work from The University of Denver. She is Phi Beta Kappa from Colorado State University.

Passionate about philanthropic and international causes, Windy supports charitable, educational, and other nonprofit programs that promote the well-being of women and children. Windy can be found on a tennis court, playing with her children, or walking her dog. She lives in Colorado with her beloved husband, three children, and her golden retriever.

Learn more: ***www.windycook.com***

FREE GIFT

My gift to you:

A FREE 30-min introductory Theta healing session

To schedule, please email Windy at **windy_beth@yahoo.com**

Featured Author

CHAPTER 2

From Rupture to Rapture

The Ecstatic Gift in Breaking Wide Open

By Lindsay Marten Ellis

As I lay here in the bath, surrounded by crimson rose petals on the eve of this watery Pisces full moon, I am once again reminded of the all-familiar feeling of sweet surrender. Approaching this memory of rupture, as tears fill my eyes, the cosmic two-by-four hits me yet again like a ton of bricks. Meeting this sacred remembrance with a warm embrace, I spend days on end gripping so tightly to the old aspects of my masked identity that were in resistance to this very moment of initiation. *I've been here before*, I tell myself as I kick and scream, resisting the very thing that will liberate me from this self-induced suffering.

And then I remember—I melt back into the ceremonial sacred bathwater, reminded again that it is merely the resistance to life's experience that creates the suffering, not the experience itself. I begin to melt into something higher as I allow the fire in my belly, the heaviness in my chest, and the resounding wave of emotions to move through me. Finally, I soften as I allow the old part of my identity to carry on with these little tiny deaths so that I can come home to more of my Divinity. Now that I am back, fully immersed in the rupture as it reverberates throughout my entire being, it is time to take it back to where the cracking wide open first began.

On the Brink of Death (Age 0-10)

Two weeks past my mama's due date, I made a fiery entrance into this world as a redheaded Virgo sun, Sagittarius rising, and Cancer moon. My soul was ready to take on the world with this cosmic trifecta of ambition, spontaneity, and heart, and that I did from the moment I landed earthside.

Then came my first initiation.

Trauma came to teach me.

It was like any other dewy Saturday morning on our back patio, riding around my favorite tricycle without a care in the world. My father ran inside when he heard my mother wailing from the kitchen of our South Florida home. She had received the mortifying news that her mother, my grandmother, transitioned in a car accident. Then BOOM, unsupervised at the ripe age of two, I rode that tricycle straight into the pool. Face down in a cyan abyss, my strawberry blonde hair floating like willows in the wind—time stood still. My entire being was in utter shock after plummeting into what felt like a vast ocean. Swimming was one of my favorite pastimes—even at that early age you could often find me splashing around in our pool. Yet, in that moment, I was paralyzed.

Our family Labrador retriever, MacGyver, bolted to the edge of the pool with a piercing bark unlike anything our family had ever witnessed. My dad's ears perked and he peered out through the sliding glass door—only to see his youngest baby floating there, unsure how long she had been face down in the water. My dad's primordial drive kicked in and he jumped into the swirling vortex to grab me and save me from the grips of death. After bringing me to dry land with no apparent impacts, my father hugged me and brought me inside to be with my mother. That is where this childhood story ends; or so I thought. Little did I know that as my mom was initiated in her own way on that very day, so was her little girl.

What's wildly fascinating about this experience is that I could not consciously recount the details until much later, yet unbeknownst to me, my body carried the memory, the trauma, and the terror for decades. Only from familial stories over the years would my brain be equipped to cognitively put together the details of this traumatic day. However, my body always knew. For most of my life, the density was trapped and stored within my emotional tissue, wreaking havoc in my physical temple.

Stored in my subconscious was deep-rooted fear, mistrust, and abandonment. Prior to that experience, purity and wonder, endless curiosity in what this majestic world had to offer, my inherently wild nature, and a strong connection to my intuition were aspects that effortlessly radiated from me. Yet after that treacherous day, the truest part of me died in that very pool and I hid Her away in the basement of my being for years to come.

Following that encounter, during my childhood years and into my youth, I slowly began to strive for perfection to avoid the story I created of getting it wrong and making mistakes. I began to value listening to everyone and everything outside myself instead of trusting my own internal compass for my highest timeline. Attempting to control everyone and everything in my environment to create the safety my inner child so desperately craved became a part of my everyday battle.

I was being pulled further and further from my eternal essence as the conditioning and programming continued to saturate me like a sponge and shape my innocent personality.

I had lost my true identity, but would I find Her again?

Traumatic Childhood Loss (Age 10-20)

Into my high school years, I continued to strive for the façade of societal success and became addicted to others' approval. Getting straight A's in high school, being Captain of the soccer team, volunteering at nursing homes, and receiving all my Catholic sacraments—I did it all for external validation.

I left my home nest for college at the age of seventeen, continuing to be influenced by all that surrounded me. I chose a cerebral, male-dominated career path in Engineering to prove to the world that a woman could "do it better." This hunger for proving myself, chasing success, and making those I loved proud through my accolades continued to fuel my personality.

Then, everything changed for me.

The night prior to my first-ever college Spring Break trip to the Bahamas was on the horizon. I spent an evening of quality time with my best friend, Nikki, and our childhood circle of friends, reminiscing and catching up. I left earlier than everyone else that evening due to my early-morning cruise departure the following day.

The next morning, I could not have been more ecstatic to arrive on the ship—the sun glistened upon the ocean waves like thousands of diamonds strewn across a blanket of deep blue hues. I felt immense peace, presence, and gratitude as we prepared to sail away.

I was pulled from that serene moment when I received a terrifying phone call that changed the trajectory of my life. I answered the phone; my dear friend Anna was crying uncontrollably and talking so fast I could barely make out a single word. Finally, after minutes of supporting her to calm her nervous system, she exclaimed, "Nikki was in a car accident last night! It's very serious, and she is in critical condition."

Upon hearing those palpable words, the horn signaled as the cruise ship left the harbor. Passing by one of the televisions on board, I noticed the accident on the screen depicting the car in shambles and the marquis that read, "Fatal Pembroke Pines accident leaves three teens in critical condition." I felt as if my life had become a horror film in which I was trapped—in the prison of my own body, with nowhere to escape but inside.

I flew back stateside the moment we reached the island and headed straight for the hospital. Seeing Nikki limp on her hospital bed made me feel like God pulled my shattered heart out of my chest and stomped all over it. Her head was shaved post-brain surgery, her face was scarred from windshield shards, and her body was bruised, battered, and broken from head to toe. She was on full life support, connected to more tubes than I could count.

Days later, after more tests and confirmation of no brain activity, the difficult decision to take Nikki off life support was made by her loving parents. I could not make sense of anything, and was utterly devastated, plagued by deep rooted emotions and sensations of grief, fear, rage, confusion, and denial crashing like thunderous waves in my body.

Questions with no logical answers began to plague my spirit. *Why her? Why not me? Why did I make it home safely that night and she did not?!* I began to question everything about my existence: the meaning of life and death, the root of my inherent belief systems, and where our eternal soul goes when our physical body dies. The idea of the Catholic God I had grown up with didn't soothe me or provide the answers I was desperately seeking. I was left feeling lost, isolated, and confused.

My parents were concerned about my grieving process and sent me to traditional therapy. Still, nothing "worked" and I fell into deeper depression. Then, Nikki's mom, Joy, miraculously passed along *Many Lives, Many Masters* by Dr. Brian Weiss. This book opened the door for me to begin to dismantle everything I knew to be true around my beliefs and indoctrinations, particularly around my Catholic upbringing. I started to follow the subtle energy of truth within my being, so that my personal relationship with God could be revealed to me.

Losing Nikki in physical form broke my heart wide open. I began to feel her presence around me viscerally the more I connected inward, and I started to grasp our eternal nature as a human species in ways I never imagined possible. The veil became thin as I felt myself, Nikki, and God as One in every moment.

Through this experience, I began to travel the world and bring more adventure into my life. I committed to spreading Nikki's ashes around the Seven Natural Wonders of the World, kicking off this journey at Australia's Great Barrier Reef. I bore witness to the miraculous in the mundane. Life began to sparkle. Magic glistened all around me.

The remainder of college was incredibly expansive as I began to come home to my true and eternal wildly loving nature. The rapture within my being began to reveal itself more and more. As I healed, the armor around my heart melted and continued to unfurl like a thousand-petaled diamond rose. I felt more at home in my body than ever before as I continued to follow the breadcrumbs of Universal Truth that resided within my sacred vessel.

I was finally home—or so I had thought.

Dis-Ease in the Body (Age 20-30)

Years later the self-induced pressures of college relentlessly infiltrated my being and I started to lose touch with my innate spiritual nature yet again. During that time, I was in and out of doctors' offices and on various medications for chronic hormone imbalance, cystic acne, adrenal fatigue, systemic stress, and beyond. My body was speaking very loudly and I wasn't listening.

As my college years had come to a close, I graduated cum laude and got hired by a reputable global engineering firm. I climbed the corporate ladder quickly and found much success in this high intensity, demanding, masculine-centric industry. Yet, my body continued to scream at me that something was seriously not right.

From the outside looking in, I had it all, but behind closed doors, I felt like I was physically at death's door. I was overworking, overcompensating, and over-consuming on every level. The approval of others began to rear its ugly head again. I wore busy like a badge of honor and completely lost touch with who I was.

Then came another threshold moment—a time when everything changed.

Following my engagement with my beloved partner Chad, a wave of peace and clarity came over me. On that very day, I declared to myself that I would reclaim autonomy and sovereignty over my body, my health, and my life during this next chapter, with my soulmate by my side.

From that day forward, I became my own advocate above all else and slowly began to call in my holistic support team with myself as my highest authority. I will never forget the day I stepped foot into my Doctor of Oriental Medicine's office and she shared, after comprehensive hormone testing, these words: "You likely will not be able to conceive a child in the future until we regulate your extremely low Progesterone hormone levels. I am sharing this as jetfuel to jumpstart your healing journey, not to initiate fear. Your body is resilient and She carries all the wisdom you need. You WILL heal." I believed her every word, and I knew she was right about my ability to heal, with her as one of my trusted guides. Newly engaged to my now-husband, I used that devastating diagnosis to light a fire in my belly and begin my empowered journey of self-healing.

I continued on this path of self-discovery and transformational healing began to happen at quantum speeds through my relationship to everything that I was consuming on a physical, emotional, energetic, and ethereal level.

Within merely six months of embarking on this holistic healing journey, I was now medication-free and had reversed all of my symptoms, after over a decade of doctors telling me this timeline would not be possible.

During this time of initiation, I began to muster up the courage to start my own consultant-based wellness business and vulnerably share my resilient story with the world, while educating, advocating, and sharing solutions using safer personal care products. I followed the strong guidance of my intuition and chose to leave corporate behind to pursue this path of truth and transparency as my life's work.

Tuning into myself brought me, yet again, the answers I had been looking for on the outside for so long. I was truly thriving and felt more alive in my body than ever before on my path as a heart-centered, soul-led entrepreneur.

I thought I had finally made it, but the Universe had other plans in store.

Dark Night of the Soul (Age 30-40)

Years into my fulfilling journey as a full-time wellness consultant, I began to feel that familiar feeling yet again. My soul was craving evolution.

There was more waiting to be discovered within me now that I was connected to my body beyond the desire to physically heal. I began to call in spiritual teachers and sisterhood communities to support the yearnings of my soul and spent two years on a path of sacred travel, intimate ceremony, and transformative retreats. During this time, I rediscovered how to connect to my highest spiritual Self while fully embodied, in the safe presence of other women.

Then came another two-by-four, hand-delivered by the Cosmos.

I remember it like yesterday. Upon returning from my first-ever journey to Hawaii sitting with sacred plants, I had my regular monthly call with my business coach at the time. I broke down in tears as a guttural shout emerged from my core and I said to her, "It is time for me to fully step into my dharma as an embodied, feminine, spiritual leader!"

It became evident that I was learning how to clear the emotional density stored within me so that I could deeply feel again, which began to open up my body as a channel for the Divine. I began to viscerally touch Source in ways I never thought possible for myself.

From this internal Knowing, I started offering private and group mentorship for women all over the world—supporting these women to heal their relationship with themselves through connecting to their bodies and claiming their Divine essence. I never felt more on purpose, nourished, and alive as I supported women awakening all over the globe.

Then I received a phone call that pulled the celestial rug out from underneath me, yet again.

Nikki's mama, Joy, called to inform me that she was terminally ill with cancer. I booked a trip following that call to visit her one final time at her North Carolina sanctuary. We spent hours in nature talking about life after death and reminiscing about our coveted mother-daughter relationship. There was a sense of warmth and serenity radiating from us both as we bundled up and connected during that white North Carolina winter.

She then asked me to help her make a holiday scrapbook for her loved ones. I said, "Of course," as she eagerly led me to a photo chest at the foot of her bed. When I opened this overflowing memory chest, a piece of papyrus paper fell right at my feet, depicting an ancient Egyptian scene. When I asked her what the scene meant or where she got it, she mentioned that a colleague made it for her many moons ago and that she had completely forgotten it was in there. She told me to keep it. A month prior to that moment, after feeling a strong impulse, I had committed to a soul pilgrimage trip to Egypt. This felt like a massive sign, but I was unclear as to its meaning. What I did know is that I had been here enough times to know that the meaning would be revealed to me when it was time.

Joy transitioned just two weeks later, and I've felt her with me ever since. Four months following her transition I headed to Egypt and brought the papyrus memento with me, folded up as a bookmark in my journal. This journey was a deep remembrance, and as I continued to heal and activate the channels in my body, I felt a deeper sense of home within me.

Towards the latter leg of our Egyptian journey, we stopped into an authentic traditional papyrus gift shop. I had no intention of purchasing anything—until I remembered Joy's keepsake. I pulled the paper out of my bag and asked our Egyptologist, Noha, to depict it for me. To my surprise, she led me to the same scene on that very wall of the shop, except I only had half the picture. The wall showcased the full scene. Queen Nefertari was shown holding hands and standing shoulder to shoulder with Goddess Isis. On the other half of the scene, Queen Nefertari was sitting gracefully on her throne merged with her Divinity, while in the presence of Goddess Maat. I knew I had to take this picture stateside with me. Immediately upon arriving home, I hung it above my altar wall.

After the trip, while in deep meditation and prayer, Goddess Isis came to me and walked me through understanding the papyrus depiction as a true representation of humanity's wholeness. She told me, *Nefertari represents our Human Self and Isis represents our Higher Self. When we surrender and link arms with the Divine within us, we merge as One. THIS is the key to healing the suffering on the planet, as it is our connection to Source that is coming back online again in this lifetime. It is only when we truly accept our humanness and embrace our holiness, that we become the bridge to create Heaven on Earth.*

It was in that moment that I fully realized that we are truly all of it. We are the human aspect of Self layered with ego, conditioning, personality, programs, and trauma; and we are the holy aspect of Self who emanates pure unconditional love and is a true fractal of God. I felt myself lock into place as this layer of my consciousness crystalized.

After losing myself for decades, at 35 years of age, I was finally HOME in my temple of wholeness.

The Rapture

I opened this sacred writing journey with you while bathing in a state of holy rupture, and it is coming to a close as I am engulfed in ecstatic rapture. As I sit and write these final musings in my lush backyard haven, the veil is thin. Mama Gaia is holding me in Her sweet embrace during this golden hour sunshower, as the sun peeks through from the Heavens.

I leave you with this naked Universal truth, wrapped up in the emotions, sensations, and earth-shattering felt experience that emerges during the integration of our soul's journey in human form.

The broken bones and the broken hearts are an integral aspect of our existence. Our pain is what allows us to feel to the depths of our being, which cracks the eternal flame of our hearts wide open. As we melt the armor that surrounds our wounds, we open ourselves to the God within and allow our Divinity to shine through.

THIS is the answer to the questions we seek.

THIS is the true meaning of life.

THIS is why we are here.

It is truly the rupture that leads to the rapture, as we co-create our individuated Heaven on Earth.

FREE GIFT

My Gift for you:

Quiz: **Discover Your Soul Blueprint & Activate Your Feminine Frequency**

A simple, fun, and enlightening 8-question quiz to unleash the whispers of your soul. You will receive clarity on your purpose, your unique key codes to embody your magic and magnetize miracles, plus rituals and practices to support your evolutionary Divine Feminine journey.

Access here: **www.lindsaymartenellis.com/quiz**

LINDSAY MARTEN ELLIS *is an embodiment guide, transformation mentor, and spiritual teacher for rising change-makers. She is also a writer, speaker, podcast hostess, Human Design facilitator, and emissary of the Divine Feminine. This former Professional Engineer traded in her accolades and to-do list for the felt experience of what it means to embrace our soul journey in human form.*

When Lindsay is not serving humanity, you can find her playing in nature with her rescue pup, Luna, traveling the world with her hubby, Chad, and dancing her prayers to George Michael's "Freedom" on the regular.

*Lindsay is a true oracle, here to leave Universal messages for the collective's evolution. You can receive her free teachings and transmissions on all major social media platforms **@lindsaymartenellis**, her podcast **Soulshine Radio**, and her website **www.lindsaymartenellis.com**.*

Featured Author

CHAPTER 3

Becoming a Radical Revolutionary

By Kathy Forest

I can still remember the first time I was assaulted by a man who said he loved me…even now 44 years later. I remember it like yesterday, what I was wearing, exactly where we were. It was 1:00 a.m. The car broke down about five miles away from our home in rural Missouri. There was no one to call at that hour even though we lived near my parents, and we were going to have to walk home. He had been drinking and I'm not exactly sure what I said that triggered him, but the punch in the face came out of nowhere and almost knocked me over. I was 20-years-old and this was the first time I had ever had anyone physically hit me. And I had never seen it either. Unlike what the statistics report, I had never even heard the term "domestic violence." I don't even know if that phrase was used at the time. The idea of a man hitting a woman, let alone a husband hitting his wife was something I did not know existed. I had never ever seen my dad hit my mom or even mistreat her. In my sheltered world, this was not "a thing." I was bewildered, shaken. And because he had been drinking, he didn't even realize he had done it. Little did I know this was only the beginning of almost three years of living hell that would ultimately shape my life and my career in oh, so many ways.

I stayed in this very abusive marriage and went through all the experiences we now define as the cycle of violence: the denial…the emotional tension…the excuses…the lies…the black eyes…being held at gunpoint…being thrown into a snowbank from a moving car while pregnant…the honeymoon phase…going back again and again and again even though I didn't want to. Nowadays, most of us know about domestic violence. We have studied it and analyzed it and even changed laws to try to assist both the victim and the abuser. And still today "every four seconds a woman dies at the hands of someone who is supposed to love her."

Luckily, I finally got out—after several close calls and countless times of leaving and returning. You may be thinking that *this* was my turning point. Maybe for a while it was. By marrying this man, I had jumped out of the fundamental Christian box that had formed and informed my life up to that point. The whole world was encouraging me to hurry and jump back in. My two-year-old daughter and I moved back in with my parents. And of course, all of us were trying to make sense of what had happened. How had a first-born "perfect child," groomed to be a "good girl," smart, top-of-her-class, sent-to-Bible-college-to-marry-a-minister-in-a-fundamental-Christian Church-tradition, how had she gone so wrong? This was the question we were ALL pondering and trying to make sense of. Because my choice to first, marry outside the church, and then, horror of horrors, get a divorce, *had not been in the plan.* This choice had rocked the world of not only this "still wet behind the ears" 20-year-old, but also my whole family and my small tight-knit home community. The image we had worked all our lives to project–a good, solid, moral Christian family—was cracking and crumbling before our eyes. What were people going to think or say? How would my father, long-time elder and Chairman of the Church Board, be perceived? All of us were trying come up with an answer. The one we finally settled on was, it was my fault. I (the victim) had made a mistake. I had picked the wrong husband. In my father's words, "It wasn't the divorce that was the sin, it was the marriage."

So, since it was my poor choice that caused all the chaos, I dutifully began my search for "the right one," and securely anchored myself back in the safe, protective fundamental Christian box. This ended about a year later. For all intents and purposes, I found "the right one," at least one that would fit neatly into that "box" with me. We were married and went on to live 11 happy years of marital bliss…kinda.

But as time went on, I once again found myself in a relationship in which I didn't have a voice, or at least not one that was respected. There was no physical hitting. But there didn't need to be. I spent the next segment of my life being the "perfect" everything—the perfect mom, wife, and student (completed my Master's degree with honors, at the top of my class, and became the Executive Director of the local Domestic Violence Shelter), the perfect boss, and the perfect employee, raising $300,000 to purchase a new state-of-the-art shelter facility. For everyone "out there," I was THE citizen against spouse abuse. My husband was the President of United Way. We were in the newspapers and in our small town were considered a (do-good-ing) power couple. At home, life was going as it always had. He made all the decisions—I did what I was told. Anything I chose to do or say or think out loud was ridiculed or belittled. Things that gave me joy were thought to seem petty and unimportant. What WAS important was that I keep show-ing up as I always did, keep being the 'good wife. Keep keeping up the ap-pearances. Keep running the shelter. Keep throwing the dinner parties. Just writing about it makes me tired.

Then I attended a seminar to learn how to teach about Emotional Abuse. And the speaking engagements began. The more I spoke about it, the more I realized that this was why "the box" was getting way too uncomfortable again. I began to see the elephant in the room: the one that had been there ALL my life. I began to realize that even though I had taken some pretty serious physical abuse in the first marriage, people didn't have to hit me to get me to do their bidding. They just had to threaten not to like me or ridicule me verbally. I had become the consummate performer and lived for approval. I truly always had. And the deep, gnawing ache inside began. Many hours of counseling later, the marriage ended. At the tender age of 38, I began a spiritual journey and adventure that would totally transform me in ways I never dreamed of. Turning point moment? Not yet. But I was getting closer.

I moved out of my small town and while I kept one foot in "the box," I began exploring all kinds of spiritual traditions. My spirituality had always been the core of who I was. But growing up, it was strictly the conservative Christianity box. Our life had been consumed by it, so much so that some thought it odd and rather cultish. My parents had sent me to Bible college in hopes that I would marry a minister. Instead, I dropped out and married my abuser. And now, here I was again, climbing out of that safe box and exploring. I was always drawn to Native American culture, so the intrigue of a "real" native Inipi (sweat lodge) ceremony drew me in. Now you must understand that at this point in my life, an outdoor girl, I absolutely was not. I would overheat when I went on a bike ride and had to be driven home, and I hated camping. So, to go into a small, enclosed area specifically to sweat made no sense for me. But I couldn't resist the spiritual draw. Something was calling me in. So, I went. During the first one, I sat by the door and was pretty uncomfortable the whole time. There were no bells or whistles, no big visions or downloads. But, unknown to me, it WAS THE BEGINNING of my new life.

The **BIG TURNING POINT** for me was my first fire walk. It was here that I literally heard Mother Earth's voice in my ears. We were told we could participate in the ceremony but not walk the hot coals if we didn't want to. Remember, I was a big chicken when it came to heat, so from the very beginning, I had intended NOT to walk— just to dance around the fire and WATCH others do it. Ha! The joke was on me. While I was walking around the fire with everyone else, for the first time ever in my life I audibly HEARD Mother's voice (not mine), saying, *"Oh yes you ARE going to walk. You are going to learn that LOVE doesn't have to hurt."* And I did. And it didn't hurt. I met the man who would become my spiritual partner and husband that night. And we went on to lead many fire walks and sweat lodges on our own property.

I would love to say it was the beginning of a "fairy-tale" life and at that moment everything changed, and I knew it. But in truth, that is not the way Mama Earth works. I knew my life had shifted but I had no idea how, or why or what it all meant. And in truth, it was a slow growing. But that first fire walk planted a seed that would take root and grow into a huge tree—a web of information and power that was in the process of re-establishing itself on this planet.

The relationship that began at that first fire walk grew into a partnership, a healing business and a non-profit ceremony site that lasted over 17 years. My husband and I both became healers. When we worked with our clients, we could see that most of the problems people were dealing with always came back to one fundamental problem—they didn't have a spiritual practice that truly fed them. They were disenchanted with church. In fact, the concept of being "sourced" spiritually—experiencing spiritual ecstasy—was a concept that eluded them and quite frankly, still does today. So, we began offering alternatives: non-traditional sweat lodges and fire walk ceremonies. At the time, that is how I saw them: alternatives to what most people thought of as spiritual practice. What I know now is that they were so much more. What we were offering people was a deep connection to the Divine through the doorway of shamanic practice. This is the root of the phrase, "As above, so below." It is the combining through our bodies, of the cosmic spiritual energy above us and the literal earth energy below us that creates magic in our lives. When we begin to make that connection through our bodies, everything changes. Things get REAL!

Now bear in mind, even though I didn't think so, I was a newbie myself, leading newer newbies. It has taken years for me to truly understand the transformation that was happening to me, my clients and students, and the planet herself, as we began to awaken these practices. To say it was the school of hard knocks is putting it very mildly. But we practiced and we learned, offering some kind of earth ceremony (a sweat lodge or fire walk) every new moon, full moon, equinox and solstice for 11 years.

It wasn't long after we started doing regular ceremonies that I added monthly women's moon-lodge circles to the mix. These led to monthly camp-outs and women's retreats, getting women on the ground as often as I could. I soon began to see that these were the most important gatherings of all, and that all the other ceremonies were done to create a safe and sacred container to hold these. I now KNOW that the knowledge and wisdom that has been resurrected from these circles *are the real reason* for all the years of ceremony work I have done. They still remain the backbone of my business and everything I do today for this fundamental reason:

The Female Body Is The Most Powerful Shamanic Tool On The Planet!

We just have never been taught how to properly care for it and use it. Most women don't know that they don't have to experience pain and suffering at the behest of their bodies once a month. They don't know that the blood their body emits once a month is not a curse but a potent and powerful elixir that can connect their body to their True Source. They don't know that their womb is more than just an incubator for babies. It is a powerful energy generator, a magnetic alchemical attraction tool. They don't realize that their bodies are so intricately tied to this planet that they literally experience all four seasons in their body every 28 days. They don't know that there is a supercharged alchemical connection between their blood, specifically their menstrual blood, and the earth that when combined, unlocks codes of power beyond their wildest imaginings. They don't know these things because they have been robbed of the most powerfully intimate and extraordinary relationship: the relationship with **their true mother**, the Earth. Most women don't know these things because we were never taught. Our mothers didn't know. Their mothers didn't know. This powerful, potent information was almost lost.

We have been brainwashed into sacrificing our body wisdom to the "gods of science" and modern ideology. We think we can manipulate our bodies and our natural cycles the same way we manipulate the weather with chem trails. But that whole system is breaking down. I don't think any of us truly realize how deep this goes, and I know we don't realize what is at stake.

Female bodies were literally designed to be conduits of Source, information, energy, power, and life-force for us, for those around us, and **FOR THIS PLANET**. Our bodies are the only ones that are open at the top and bottom. Indigenous peoples knew this. They honored, revered, and protected their women for this very reason. It is no accident that when women were deeply connected to the earth, this planet flourished for thousands of years. It is only in the past few centuries that we have seen a rapid decline.

Years ago, I received a beautiful download from Mary Magdalene. Here's a tiny part of it…

*"The information—the tools—necessary to make
the radical shift needed on this planet in a
a very short period of time is housed
within the wombs of women of this age.
You have the ability to heal your planet and
save your world. It is up to you.
Do you desire to keep this beautiful haven a
safe place for the next seven generations and
beyond? Do you desire a place for your
children to grow and learn? It is up to you."*

When we think of the daunting tasks ahead of us, it would be very easy to become overwhelmed or to want to blame men, patriarchy, or some other evil force "out there." But I am convinced that the answer is quite simple. If enough women remember, if enough women re-establish their relationship with their bodies, their cycles, and their true Mother, we can turn the tide. We can harvest the information housed inside our bodies. We can make the necessary changes.

When I look back on this powerful transformation that has taken over two decades, the difference is like night and day. I went from a weak, sickly, scared-of-her-own-shadow girl to a powerful shamaness and leader of women all over the world—a woman who would rather be barefoot outside or in a sweat lodge than anywhere else. Mom (the Earth Mother) came and found me. She sought me. But the pain and suffering I went through to find her was totally unnecessary. All the experiences of both myself and all those around me, I believe, are part of a bigger, broader problem. They are symptoms of a world that has been totally separated from its Mother. I am convinced that most of the difficulties our world is facing right now could be tempered or totally alleviated if women were empowered to develop their deep relationship with the planet we live on. And, quite frankly, we don't have time for all of us to take twenty years to learn it. We don't have time for us to be convinced or coaxed or coddled into it. We simply must make the necessary changes now.

Join a circle. Find a group of women you resonate with and gather with them once a month, maybe around the new moon or full moon...and

WATCH THE MAGIC HAPPEN. The solutions to all the challenges we face are as close as our breath.

So, no—I never became a fundamental Christian minister's wife—lucky for them!

I became the beginning of a revolution.

I became a healer of women.

I became the beginning of the restoration of the New Earth.

FREE GIFT

My Free Gift to You:

Pillars of the Feminine Mysteries: Stalking the Goddess in the 21st Century

A 7-Module Course designed to give you all the tools and information you need to remember...how to get your body back and use it as it was intended...how to mine it for the information you right now may desperately need to get your life back on track!

Visit **www.celestialforestinstitute.com/copy-of-cct-landing-page**

Kathy Forest, MS, CHt, *is a seasoned ceremony leader and wild-woman High Priestess. She has been using her skill as a psychotherapist, and master healer and her extensive knowledge of the human energy field to assist women (and the men who love them) to deeply transform their lives through soul healing down to the cellular level for over 30 years. She began her work in feminine empowerment as the Executive Director of a Domestic Violence shelter in central Missouri. She was very active in the Missouri Coalition Against Domestic Violence and established a state-of-the-art shelter facility and domestic violence recovery program in her hometown 25 years ago.*

Kathy is an alchemical change agent. She is skilled at diving deep, getting to the root cause of any difficulty and transforming it with compassion and grace. She is an advocate and catalyst for deep womb healing, and helps women access their birthright of running clear, clean and current Shakti Life Force energy through their bodies. She offers women a variety of healing, growth and educational opportunities via on-line women's circles, Priestess and Energy healing trainings, and deep dives into the Feminine Mysteries through in-person retreats. She also offers private healing and coaching sessions. Her goal is to empower women "to do what they came to this planet to do."

She is the founder and owner of Celestial Forest Institute of Energy Healing and Shamanic Studies.

Learn more: **www.celestialforestinstitute.com**

Featured Author

CHAPTER 4

Hell, No

By Lara O'Neil

There was a period in my life when I felt like I had a split personality. Not full-blown Sybil stuff, but troublesome, nonetheless. I put on my game face at work to fulfill my role but was a different person in my heart and home. I was working in a traditional allopathic pediatric office and seeing patients every ten to fifteen minutes, working in a model of care where "wellness visits" were focused primarily on vaccinations, and symptoms of illness were mostly treated with medications. These are important parts of pediatric care, but there was little individuality taken into account, or investigation of root causes. Nor was there much consideration of culture, religion, or values. There simply wasn't enough time in this type of care. Children seemed to be getting sicker, and there was more chronic disease. Quantity rather than quality of care was emphasized. The culture of the office was racist, conformist, and toxic. I felt trapped in a patriarchal system of medicine, insurance, and big pharma.

I loved what I did, but I wanted to give more, help more, make more of a difference. I dreamed of finding another job in integrative and holistic medicine, where I could practice the way I wanted to, the way my heart yearned to—the way I took care of myself and my own children. I had many patients who chose to see me, and they, too, longed for this type of care. I did the best I could within the constraints of my role, thoroughly enjoying these moments, especially when I felt I had really made a difference or positive impact.

Even though I wasn't satisfied with my career, I was a single mom with three young children, and felt I needed the security that came with good income and benefits. I had worked hard and invested in a lot of schooling to get where I was. I struggled with feelings of inadequacy, frustration, and shame. I dreamed of the "knight in shining armor" who would offer me my dream job. But years went by, and guess what, that never happened.

During those years, whenever I wasn't at work, I filled any possible free time I had by developing a meditation practice and going to yoga classes and retreats. I went to integrative healers for myself and my children and chose natural therapies when possible. I took classes, seminars, and workshops and read everything I could about integrative medicine, natural remedies, and holistic health. During these disjointed times, I was happy and content. But then I would go to work and feel miserable, almost like an imposter. I knew that when there is a division like this, you are not as good or effective at either aspect of life. I became progressively miserable, stressed, and exhausted. I was short-tempered with my children and disappointed with myself. Yet over the course of another few years, I was becoming increasingly longing, increasingly curious, increasingly bold. Something was stewing in me.

The final straw was a morning I remember vividly. The day before, at a lunchtime staff meeting, my coworkers were belaboring about an incident when I was running twenty minutes behind. This happened all the time with the other doctors—not just me—but for some reason, they had to turn my tardiness into a long conversation that day and vilify me. I was an excellent employee, well-liked by the patients, and had been working there for nine years. Sick to my stomach, I sat there and said nothing. I had been running late because the fifteen minutes set aside to see the patient was not nearly enough.

I cried the entire twenty-minute drive to work the next morning. It wasn't about the staff meeting the day before, but a long list of culminating events over years. My work was soul-crushing. I wanted to help children and their families, but how could I do this if I couldn't even help myself? Looking back, it had been a release. In that moment I realized—I knew from the bottom of my soul—that I could no longer do this! What was I thinking?!?! This job had become a HELL NO.

I chose to take a leap of faith, follow my heart and desires, leave my job and go out on my own. But don't get me wrong, it was terrifying. I doubted myself. I was sick with fear about being able to financially support myself and my children. I cried about the families and patients I would be leaving. I had many sleepless nights. But the funny thing is, even despite all this, I also knew from a deeper place that I was 100% doing the right thing. I was being called to find my purpose in soul-driven work. So, I began the process of alchemizing the two worlds I was living in.

I have studied, experienced, and have been thoroughly intrigued by energy healing since the early 90s, with my first exposure in undergraduate nursing school. The most memorable part of these four years of schooling was the mere two hours we spent learning about "Therapeutic Touch" developed by Delores Krieger PhD, RN in the 1970s. The world of energy healing can be difficult to analyze and discuss because it is cosmic and mysterious in nature. I know the science, research, and literature is in vast support of it, but for me, it is not as important, because it is experiential. My first phase of branching out of the traditional medical training that I had received, was enrolling in a Reiki healing training course. The experience was one of my biggest steps towards my love and dedication to alternative healing practices. Using Reiki regularly on myself and sometimes on my children, I have come to know the deep rewards on a subtle energetic level. I remain in awe of how the human body can have so many complicated, intricate structures all working systematically within one system of balance and regulation.

My trainings in Cranial Sacral Therapy (CST) through Upledger Institute led me to an even deeper understanding of how the intricacies of the body in its entirety are all connected and all energy. Everything affects everything else. This is universally true as well. My favorite Native American proverb from Chief Seattle in 1854 hangs in my bedroom as it resonates so profoundly: *"Humankind has not woven the web of life. We are but one thread within it. Whatever we do to the web, we do to ourselves. All things are bound together. All things connect."*

Chinese medicine also has a beautiful understanding of how emotional, physical, and spiritual dynamics organize us. Acupuncture and Chinese medicine are designed to support qi, or life force, to flow freely in the body, thereby reducing physical disease and disharmony. In harmony we have health, in disharmony we have dis-ease and suffering, unlike Western medicine which is rooted in looking at the body and disease in parts, organs, and symptoms that are identified and treated separately.

In Dr. Robert Mendelsohn's acclaimed and controversial book, *How to Raise a Healthy Child, In Spite of Your Doctor,* he talks about not going to your pediatrician when your child is sick. The man had some valid points! He clearly saw the limitations of Western medicine, especially in primary care. Even though you could say he was talking himself out of a career. He was a brilliant doctor, and I admire his spirit and willingness to be a well-known maverick in the medical profession. But what Dr. Mendelsohn knew nothing about was integrative medicine and what it can offer. If he did, perhaps his book would be…How to Raise a Healthy Child, in Partnership with Your Doctor.

I have an incredible amount of respect for healthcare providers and medical doctors. They are smart, admirable, have a passion for helping people, and are by and large committed to their mission. I am truly grateful for healthcare systems, which are on the front lines and provide cutting-edge, lifesaving medications and interventions. I have had many patients that have greatly benefited from this. Unfortunately, the healthcare industry in general has deep-rooted, limiting issues, driven by profit and one-size-fits-all algorithms. I also see a pattern of over-medicalization stemming from fear of liability. Doctors and providers often get absorbed into a system they don't fully see—one where political motivations, insurance companies, and pharmaceutical corporations have way too much power, influence, and financial gains. The algorithms and guidelines are the same for everyone; if the doctor didn't learn about it in medical school, then it doesn't exist, or is labeled misinformation or quackery. Yet I believe strongly in respecting that science is always evolving, as well as the importance of individuality and individual choice. What is labeled as misinformation today, may be truth tomorrow, or vice versa.

Western medicine's focus on killing this bug, removing that bad thing, stopping these symptoms—doesn't resonate with me. At least not all the time. However, in this current world, where polarization is seemingly worse than ever before, I feel a powerful call to drop the arms and work together. Both allopathic and holistic healthcare are valuable and meaningful. We don't have to throw the baby out with the bath water, so to speak. There is power in using both, depending on what is needed. Both ways deserve respect. This is what integrative medicine truly is. I believe in the body's innate ability to heal with nurturing and listening. I am also a curious, open scientist who is always willing to learn and consider.

I grew up Quaker, thanks to my hippie parents who went to college in the 60s, found each other during this historical time of rebellion and the Vietnam War, veered away from their conservative Christian upbringing full of doctrine, and found Quakerism together. As I reflect on integrative medicine, I am struck by some of its parallels with the philosophy and birth of Quakerism. The religion was founded in the 17th century by George Fox, during a time of religious turmoil in England with people seeking reform. Fox believed that the presence of God was found not just in churches, but within people. Even though his views were shared by many, and the movement was growing, he was seen by some as a threat to society and was jailed for blasphemy in 1650. Quaker views were considered radical, such as the idea that men and women were spiritual equals. They believed that we are all equal in the eyes of God. They were a pivotal part in the women's suffrage movement as well as the fight to abolish slavery. The dedication has continued, and many modern-day Quakers are still championing for social injustice and human rights. In Quaker services, there is no minister. You sit in silent worship. You are your own connection to the spirit. They believe in an individual's "inner light," or conscience, to guide their spiritual connection. You can speak if you feel moved to during worship. The religion attracts all kinds of people because of their righteous belief in acceptance.

Integrative medicine is not a rejection of science and medical advances, but rather a deepened investigation into things that medical science may not be fully explaining. It is also recognition of what science already fully understands but may overlook or devalue in our fast-paced current healthcare crisis. Human needs are not a "one-size-fits-all" category. Since every person's biochemistry is uniquely different, what works for one person is not always going to work for the next. This contradicts a Western doctor's training to give "this medicine for that disease," or to "administer this test to diagnose that problem." The concept that the body can heal itself is vital, profound, and real. Health and healing should be an interaction or interplay between client and healer. This can threaten traditional medical training, which emphasizes the cavalier heroic doctor who is needed to treat the sick. Quakers didn't reject Christianity, yet they rejected the constraints of their religious expression and pressure to bow to the Church of England. They faced fear of persecution, torture, and imprisonment, but remained steadfast in their beliefs, flourished, and created new ways of thinking and living.

When I was working in the traditional setting, I was productive and an achiever, but felt like a factory worker and therefore was dissatisfied. I was now ready to emerge as a more authentic version of myself. I needed to reclaim myself. It was my feminine reclamation.

When I decided to "set up shop" on my own, I was talking to a dear friend of mine, who was also a pediatric provider. She asked me, "What do you want your office to be like? Why are you really doing this?" I started to rattle off all the things I didn't want for my practice, and the list was getting pretty long. She stopped me and said "No, don't tell me what you don't want, envision what you DO want!" That made me pause and reframe. It became clear to me that what I really wanted was a pediatric office that families want to come to! Where they actually look forward to sharing their health journeys with me. Where their kids feel safe, loved, and nurtured. A place where families of all races, religions, cultures, values, and choices can come and feel accepted, valued, and free to have open discussions. I know what it is like to feel misunderstood, unseen, and afraid to speak your truth. I never want children to have to go through that or feel that way—not on my watch. I wanted an office where I could really make a difference in the health and vitality of these children and their families. It felt liberating and exciting to have this clarity, and I was off and running!

I have learned—albeit the hard way—that whenever you make a big piv-ot in your life to follow your heart and soul's purpose, it is never easy. Dis-rupting the status quo—lovingly called the "Big Snooze" in Jen Sincero's *You Are a Badass*—is usually followed by chaos. It almost feels like the universe is testing you to make sure you really got this. The ego vehemently does not like change. It is a journey of fortitude, perseverance, and faith. I ex-perienced this after my divorce when I had three young children. First, the sewage drain clogged and my basement literally filled up with shit. A few months later, when I went downstairs to make breakfast for the girls before getting them to school and rushing to work, I discovered that the ceiling had fallen on top of my kitchen table. I was paralyzed with overwhelm. Yup, I hear you chuckling, I know you know what I am talking about. Years later, after I opened my business in integrative medicine, I became very ill with Lyme disease for over six months but still needed to run the practice and see patients. Then COVID hit and we were faced with great uncertainty with what was in front of us, as well as for the future of our small private busi-ness. A few months later my business partner faced an unspeakable horrific family tragedy, and a few months after that—I did as well. I am so grateful for my knowledge and faith in holistic medicine for spiritual, emotional, and physical healing that supported me through these challenging times.

As I am writing this, I have a successful, busy integrative practice and feel blessed. Yet it has been full of trials and tribulations, blood, sweat, tears, and many curve-balls. Some days I feel disheartened. Other days I remem-ber that this is what I have always wanted, didn't think I could ever have, and have worked very hard for. On those days I feel aligned with my di-vine purpose and truly grateful. Some days I am full of righteous rage and disgust towards the healthcare industry, the health insurance industry, and the pharmaceutical industry, as well as the resulting entitlements from con-sumers. Other days I am filled with love for my patients and what I can offer them. I get to feel all the joy and all the suffering. The more I feel, the more I grow. I wouldn't have it any other way.

As I am now freshly past the sacrificial time of having young children at home and entering into a new phase of "empty nester" and menopause, I find that my focus, desires, truths, and passions are evolving and expanding. I am more ready to share, speak, and be seen in my truth and authenticity in a whole new way. I have matured from a young rebel who saw a problem, to a committed leader for the long haul. Bucking against a broken system doesn't always work; we need devotion full of love and vision. I see my path now to be a part of the growing pioneer movement for the future of our healthcare industry.

As I enter another turning point of my own anthology, turning 2.0, so to speak, I am faced again with challenges of impending burnout and abandoning self. I balance it with continued nurturing of myself and the services I offer. I am running a business and providing care to patients, continuing to find ways to support myself while providing the care and service that I know is my soul's purpose. I am working to create something sustainable, replicable, productive, and nourishing.

It is shocking and heartbreaking to look at the statistics around burnout, abandonment, and even suicide among healthcare providers. I am constantly refocusing and working to become the master of my own energy and vitality so that I can serve others more effectively, and I hope to support other providers of all kinds to do the same. Healthcare providers are only human and need nourishing, healing, and sustaining, too, after all. I revere the motto, "Healers heal thyself." This includes caregivers and parents. Sometimes I feel I am failing in this area, and sometimes I do quite well, but either way, it is important to me to "walk the talk" and lead by example. It is common for care providers and healers to struggle with creating boundaries and honoring themselves and their professional knowledge and skills as valuable. There is a fine line between doing whatever you can to help another in need and abandoning your own sovereignty. I bring forth a protocol for healthcare providers as well as other leaders and coaches:

1. *Do not be afraid to have boundaries. As caregivers, it can feel like going "against your grain." But it is important to know our own limits, within a loving construct, or you will be at risk of burnout, growing bitter, and being of no good to anyone!*

2. *There is nothing shameful in charging for the value of your services and time. You are worth it! Money is an exchange of energy and if you are constantly devaluing your services, then it will ultimately reduce the quality of your care.*

3. *Take time off and do things that you love. Nurture yourself on a regular basis. To be healthy, vital, and whole in the best way you can, is one of the greatest things you can do for your patients. Embody your leadership and service. "My cup runneth over"—you are not able to give as well when you are depleted.*

4. *Be easy on yourself. You may have mishaps or slip-ups in all these areas. We are only human. With love in our hearts, willingness to learn, and remaining curious and open, there are really no mistakes.*

5. *In moments when you lose sight of your vision and feel stressed, overwhelmed, sad, or angry, gently remind yourself, yes, these feeling are valid, as well as, what a gift it is to be able to serve others in the way of the healer.*

This is my story. I hope it inspires you. I hope it is thought-provoking. If you are a healthcare provider or healer who wants to provide care in a better way, and are frustrated by the current healthcare system, we need you, and I have faith in you! If you are a parent and want healthcare for your child that feels like it has your family's best interest at heart, then you can absolutely have that! I wrote this with you in mind. We need change. We deserve better. Let's do this together. Let's make this a "Hell, Yes!"

> *"I believe the children are our future, teach them well and let them lead the way. Show them all the beauty they possess inside"*
>
> —Whitney Houston/Linda Creed

Lara O'Neil, APRN, CPNP *is the author of* Rescuing Ourselves: How Integrative Medicine Improved the Lives of Myself, My Children, And My Patients *releasing in the fall of 2023. Through this personal transformation journey, shared expertise and vision, one can clearly see the future of a better healthcare system that values the body, mind and soul. Explored through the lens of authenticity, vulnerability, passion and a deep love for her work, the reader will find themselves immersed in the journey with Lara, and find themselves laughing to crying and everything in-between, but most of all, hopeful.*

Lara has over 25 years working with children and their families. She has had the privilege of experiences in home care, hospitals, school settings, primary care pediatric office, and now owning her own thriving integrative pediatric and family wellness center. She is an author, a healer, and a sought after and respected pediatric provider. She is a Certified Pediatric Nurse Practitioner with her Masters in Arts from the College of St. Catherine in St Paul, Minnesota. She has completed additional certification in Integrative Health and Healing, as well as Cranial Sacral Therapy and Reiki healing.

Yoga and meditation are a sacred part of her daily life, and also enjoys biking, hiking, and being in or near the ocean. She is a passionate and fierce protector of all things innocent, animals, children and the earth.

She lives in Connecticut with her 3 uniquely different daughters, 2 eccentric cats, and her lifetime partner.

*Learn more at **thrivecenterforhealth.com** or **laraoneil.com***

FREE GIFT

My Free Gift to You:

Walking Meditation and Guided Visualization

An audio walking meditation and guided visualization for building the holistic practice of your dreams.

To access, please visit **www.laraoneil.com**

Featured Author

CHAPTER 5

Raison d'être

The New Adventures of the Black Girl in Her Search for God

By Cydya Smith

*rai·son d'ê·tre| rāzôn detre | noun) the most important reason or purpose for someone or something's existence.

I stumbled into the room I shared with my sister and my great-grandmother. The relief I felt at finding myself alone was great. I heard and felt my heart pounding in my head. I couldn't catch my breath. My reflection in the mirror facing the door I had closed and was now leaning against, was of me with my mouth open, gasping. I sat down on great granny's bed and closed my eyes, but felt dizzy, then nauseous—so I opened them quickly and sank down to the floor with my back against the bed. I was holding on to the hem of great granny's pink chenille bedspread trying to catch my breath.

Suddenly I was breathing easier. The cacophonous heartbeat inside my head echoing the hammering inside my chest gradually slowed until I remembered what had precipitated my first turning point event. An event when "time stood still;" an event I knew that I would never forget.

I had come inside from playing and heard my mother crying. This was strange, so I stopped and listened quietly. Someone dear had died, and she was concerned about how to tell us. My father said that we had to learn that everyone dies eventually. I only heard "everyone dies" and this meant that I too was going to die. One day I would no longer be—but where would I be? This was too much to think about, so I panicked. Mother found me there, sitting on the floor and she gathered me up in her arms and whispered to me who had died, who we would never see again. I was nine.

I am now just days away from my 41st birthday and have been driving all night. Anticipation and resolve are the blended fuels propelling me forward. I confess to being excited beyond measure to be off on this adventure—this quest for answers to the meaning of life…my life, specifically.

I had embarked upon an intentional meditation practice and partial fast that would last for 40 days and 40 nights. In despair I had alternately pleaded as well as demanded tangible proof from the Universe to answer my query; something specific and irrefutable that would leave no doubt that my query was acknowledged. Every sinew in my soul yearned for answers and I'd planned my adventure with minute detail to culminate on the 39th and 40th day to meditate at my normal time, from 5 to 6 a.m., on Mount Shasta, California, the place I was now driving to.

However, in reaching this major turning point in my life, I needed to access memory and attempt to perceive, what had compelled me to go on this quest? Why was I so intent on answers?

Several childhood incidents emerged as I backpedaled through my memory. I recalled how I felt when I overheard that a beloved cousin, who was my age, had died, and the feelings came rushing back. My heart felt as if it would burst, and it was difficult to breathe as my mind skittered across thoughts of being dead myself, questioning, where would I go when I was no longer alive? No longer "Me?"

This memory flowed into another, of my being deathly ill as a child. I was in great granny's bed—the shades were drawn because the light hurt. I felt cold cloths on my forehead—I was hot, but I was shivering. I heard the hushed voices, the frequent "shushing" to my siblings, and great granny reading to me from her Bible. I believed that she was reading to me from her Bible because I must be dying. I don't remember being afraid, but the sound of her gentle voice reading the endless litany of "begats" made me anxious, so I interrupted fretfully and asked, "Granny, who begat God?" Even in my feverish state I observed her countenance shift and felt the hint of rebuke as she scolded, "You're not supposed to ask that baby." After a perplexed gaze at me, she continued. But my mind raced off as I began to ponder in that moment, (yes… another one of those "moments") that if I didn't die, I was going to know all I could know about "God."

During the time of my illness, I awakened one night to the sound of a voice and the vision of a shimmering presence floating around my bed. It was magical. My body tingled all over as waves of wonderfulness flowed over me and a comforting voice spoke, saying: "Beloved, you must stay!" These words reverberated inside my head as the shimmering presence faded away. After that, I began to get well.

I wouldn't see the shimmering presence again, but in certain moments, encouraging words resonated inside my head as a reminder that it is ever present.

So now, here I am, driving toward the greatest adventure of my life. I'd read Mayan Factor by Jose Arguelles. He and his wife, Lloydine, conceived a global event, inviting everyone on the planet to visit any sacred site in August 1987 to meditate for world peace while simultaneously heralding the dawning of the Age of Aquarius. I was over all the moons of Jupiter after learning that a sacred site was within driving distance from me—only 600 miles! My pilgrimage would take me from Los Angeles to Mount Shasta, where I could participate in the first Harmonic Convergence on August 16th-17th, 1987, joining with others to meditate for world peace and simultaneously receive an answer to my query. A wonder-filled birthday gift to myself. So, fortified with essentials, a full tank of gas, and my self-curated "driving music," I journeyed eagerly and expectantly into the night.

We were Episcopalians. My father was a lay reader, my brother—an acolyte, and my mother, sister, and I sang in the choirs. It was inspiring, belonging to a sacred space, learning the liturgy, singing beautiful music, and making a familial contribution within that space. Inside me were many unformed questions (my father said I asked too many questions sometimes) but the hunger to seek answers had given way to other childhood pursuits.

One idyllic summer, my siblings and I attended vacation Bible school to learn the Parables. Parents and friends would be invited to a showcase at summer's end. Our priest, Father Williams, assigned me the part of Jesus, the narrator of the showcase. The other children would act out each parable. I worried and asked Father Williams during rehearsal how I could act the part of Jesus, since I was being teased about it. Father Williams stopped rehearsal and explained that it was perfectly acceptable for me to narrate because he needed the best reader in the group to have the responsibility of narrating. He then went on to explain that Jesus was a teacher who, by impeccable example, taught that each of us can do what he did by learning and practicing his teachings. He smiled and advised me and the others to learn our parts well and not to worry. We were a hit!

Then, when I was thirteen—upheaval! Our family moved across the country from Detroit, Michigan to Tucson, Arizona, where my mother's family lived. We were suddenly adrift in an unknown sea until we found an Episcopal church, where we, as the first African American family, were welcomed, so, breathing a collective sigh of relief, we gratefully resumed the same roles as before.

My parents obtained work that allowed them to flourish. My father's work often cast him into the limelight, where, as his family, we could also shine. In summer months, our family participated in summer stock productions at the University of Arizona, and it was during that time that I knew I wanted to study acting.

During my senior year in high school, however, father announced that he'd been offered a posting as a Cadet in the Episcopal Church Army, which meant we'd be moving again, this time to Dallas, Texas, where he'd be pastor of a church. Nothing I could say would induce him to allow me to stay in Arizona to study acting. I was heartbroken and became rebellious.

In Texas, I left college after one year, much to my father's displeasure. He'd insisted that I enroll in the college where he held a chaplaincy. The college had no drama department, and I was not challenged by the curriculum.

So, it was during one of those castigating rants my father subjected me to, saying that I was destined to fail in life if I didn't have a college degree, that I finally responded with clever, over-confident, youthful flippancy and said, "Don't worry, I'll educate myself in all things that interest me, and I'll have several Ph.D.'s in experience from the University of Life before I die." His frustration was apoplectic, and he looked as if he would hit me. Mother's intuitiveness intervened, and she decided I should stay for a brief period at the home of her great uncle and his family in Houston. I rejoiced that finally I would have some freedom to make my own decisions.

In Houston, I got a job at the post office, helped my great aunt clean houses, and enrolled in the "John Robert Powers" modeling school (where I was an anomaly). I missed my family terribly though, and my father wrote several times asking me to come home. After a year I relented and moved back to Dallas. I found a job in retail, not modeling as I'd hoped, and resigned myself to attending church with family while prospecting for my future.

Ironically, my father championed the idea of my becoming a flight attendant as he had not to my becoming an actress. So, my young adult years found me based in New York City as a flight attendant. Shortly after my move to New York, my father was promoted to National Director of the Episcopal Church Army HQ in New York City. So, I still found myself under the watchful, albeit nurturing gaze of my family. I took courses at the Actors Studio, and at The New School, and thoroughly enjoyed New York.

The comforting voice seemed to be on hiatus, and honestly, I didn't listen for it because I was blossoming in a world that continuously bloomed for me in Technicolor and stereophonic sound. I traveled, curiously. I wanted to get as far away from the continental United States as possible—untethered—so the world would be my backdrop, and I marveled at the amazing people I met while experiencing different cultures in the various cities, states, and countries I traveled to. I was enchanted with the world, and the world seemed equally enchanted with me.

Fast forward ten years—I'd been selected to represent my airline as the principal in a series of national television commercials, print ads, and other special assignments, and now lived in Los Angeles, where the company had relocated me. I bought a car and a condominium. I had already become a pet parent in New York when I rescued a puppy and was gifted with a kitten from a neighbor who lived in my building in Los Angeles. My beautiful female animal family! I took writing and acting classes and made friends of people with shared interests who introduced me to other interesting people and experiences, which ran the gamut from meeting and drinking champagne with Mikael Baryshnikov and others backstage at the Los Angeles Philharmonic after a performance, to being introduced to Carlos Castaneda after his lecture at UCLA. Carlos invited my friends and I to a talk he was giving at a college bookstore in Westwood, and he subsequently invited me to become part of what he called a "spiritual warrior" group. I respectfully declined.

I also experienced my first total devastation when my mother died in New York, and I couldn't be with her. How could "God" let her die in such agony? My guilt for not being there, was the impetus that launched me, somewhat angrily, but with focused intent, back to the mindset of that questioning child—back onto a spiritual path that had been obscured by the illusion of the life I was thoughtlessly creating. The path had always been backstage, waiting in the wings, and it would now come full circle to bask in the encouraging, loving light of my soul.

I began reading voraciously and intentionally, adding books on philosophy and various religions to my library. I purchased a slim, first-edition book by George Bernard Shaw called: The Adventures of the Black Girl in Her Search for God at a local flea market and thought this a particularly propitious purchase and decided that I would title my story: The NEW Adventures of the Black Girl in Her Search for God.

I also acquired *The Secret Teachings of All Ages* by Manley P. Hall, after having seen it prominently displayed at a respected friend's apartment in New York. WOW! Also, and by fortunate happenstance, I found an English edition of *The Meditations of Marcus Aurelius* on a train while traveling from Rome to Florence. It began to feel like I was keeping the promise made to my father to truly educate myself. Then…a snafu hit my timeline!

An acquaintance invited me to accompany her to the Playboy Mansion where I observed myself being seduced into a pseudo-glamorous world. Every Sunday, dressed to impress, we'd excursion to the mansion for "Movie Night with Hef." However, what was initially exhilarating soon became empty and appalling. One Sunday while listlessly selecting what to wear, a character in a film on television began to sing "Amazing Grace." Suddenly (here comes one of the turning point moments again), confusion and desolation overcame me. I unraveled, and surrendering in despair, sank miserably to my knees. I evaporated, sobbing, pleading with upstretched arms, "God, Please Help Me! Who am I? What is the meaning of life? Why am I here?" I cried to exhaustion; yet somehow, I arose feeling light-hearted…and snap!—the Playboy Mansion distraction faded into the past.

I enrolled in a "Soul Pursuit" course at the Metaphysical Institute. The extensive reading list included books by Blavatsky among others, and Thoth's Emerald Tablet. I learned to meditate, studied crystals, achieved a second degree in Reiki, and worked with flower essences to successfully heal myself of a nicotine addiction. I had vivid dreams, one in which a white dove sat in my hand and told me that I would have my "heart's desire." The famous Bodhi Tree Bookstore, a few blocks from where I lived, became my haven and is where I'd purchased *Mayan Factor.*

Full circle to now, as I'm driving through the night, determined to be on time. Everything had fallen into place perfectly for my trip to Mount Shasta. All hotels, motels, and campsites were booked, but in delightful synchronicity, while on assignment at the airport, a friendly, animated woman named Pauli, checking in for her flight, said she was from Mount Shasta City and as I explained my plight while issuing her boarding pass, she graciously invited me to stay with her.

I drove into Mount Shasta City thirty minutes before my meditation time. Using my compass, I scoped out a secluded area with trees facing east and pulled over for my morning meditation—right on time. Afterward, I drove to a diner and slept two hours in the brightly lit parking lot.

Pauli's apartment was easy to find. I arrived around 10 a.m. to shower and change. We adventured out and I treated us to a splendid brunch. Then, we walked up beyond the base of the mountain to connect with others who'd gathered in the heady, festive atmosphere. Later, coming down from the mountain, we meandered through colorful venues, admiring and snacking. We ended the day at a Tibetan Bowl concert in a tiny church, marveling at the fact that the evocative tones the bowls made caused the chandeliers to sway.

Weary though merry, we returned to Pauli's. She invited me to meditate with her the next morning. I murmured that I would, as my head gratefully nestled into the pillow.

"BELOVED, WAKE UP!" My eyes opened. "WAKE UP!" The voice inside my head was shouting urgently. The clock showed 5:55, meaning I'd slept through most of my meditation time. Panicked, I bolted upright in bed and was instantly grasped into an exquisite, pulsating embrace of violet light! It felt like electronic beams of amplified bliss, caressing me with cascading waves of love, like what I'd experienced as a child, but increased to the millionth degree. My body was saturated in a delicious effusion—I smelled and tasted violets. The color violet continuously spiraled on a loop inside me, drenching my cells, penetrating through skin, bones, and marrow. I tingled all over and heard myself moaning. Then abruptly—the embrace ended. The time was still 5:55, yet it'd felt like an eternity. Time stood still! I burrowed under the covers in breathless astonishment. Later, I heard Pauli knock at my door, but I couldn't speak. She opened the door and whispered: "You awake?" When I found my voice, I shared what I'd experienced. She gripped the doorknob tightly, and clutching her chest, she gasped: "Oh my God! It's Saint Germain!"

"Who?" I croaked.

"My dear!" Pauli exclaimed, coming to hug me, "He's the Patron Saint of the New Age, Cohan of the Seventh Ray, Lord of the Ascension! Oh, My!" she repeated.

I was crestfallen, questioning...Saint Germain? Not God? Violets? Ascension? What is this? The drive home was hazy. The next day after work, I escaped to the Bodhi Tree—to the solace of my alcove. I allowed my gaze to roam about the shelves until it cast upon a slim lavender volume on an adjacent shelf that seemed to beckon me. My body tingled as I reached for it and read the words on the spine: *Violet Fire* on top—Saint Germain on the bottom. WOW! My heart expanded in gratitude, grace, and above all—WONDER.

During the next Soul Pursuit class, I recounted my experience. The teacher's homework for me was a handwritten note stating: *Those gifted with the Violet Fire must read St. John, Chapter 14, Verse 26 in the Bible.*

Once home, I dusted off great granny's Bible and read:

"But the 'Comforter,' which is the Holy Ghost,
whom the Father will send in my name, he shall
teach you all things, and bring all things to your
remembrance, whatsoever I have said unto you."

This was acknowledgment—a specific answer to my query.

That night in a dream, I was ascending staircases in a dark house. On the top step of the seventh staircase was a jewelry box containing a necklace of sparkling green gemstones. I believe that each green stone on that necklace represents one of those moments when "time stood still" and became major turning points for me.

I studied Hermetic Philosophy for twenty years with people from all over the world and was initiated in an underground temple in South America. My father lived long enough to take pride in my accomplishments and know that I was well-educated because of the way I choose to live my life…not by having a college degree.

The comforting voice returned, frequently awakening me from sleep to download words that eventually become poems. The poem on the next page provided answers to my query, "Who I am, Why I am here, and Why we are all here":

Raison d'être

You've slipped through the portal
From a different place
Where there are no illusions
To discern, decipher, then definitively discard
This dimension's manipulative
Seductively mesmerizing delusions

Awake Divinity!
You are Heaven's child
You did not incarnate merely to survive
Seek within
Humbly demand to remember
Why you chose this time to be alive

Act on this! The future is now!
Prepare to quantum leap
As life escalates the pace
For you were charged before birth
Honor bound and with soul intent
To become the Stellar Human Race

© Cydya Smith

CYDYA SMITH *was honored with the Distinguished Service Award for Merit by American Airlines, and she was invited to record one of her poems for the video archive of the Institute of Noetic Sciences (IONS). She moderated several dialogues between community activists and the NYPD to aid in the development of the Courtesy, Professionalism and Respect (CPR) campaign. She was then selected to create and teach Stress Management workshops annually for the Executive Development Department of the New York Police Academy.*

She created the award-winning recruitment book for the U.S. Department of Labor's million-dollar Banking Training Program grant for City University of New York. She taught Time Management, Emotional Intelligence, Listening Skills, The Seven Habits of Highly Effective People for Verizon, and The Principles of Management for Mount Sinai Hospital's Adult Education Program.

Cydya is also a Health Counselor, certified by Teachers College and the American Association of Drugless Practitioners (AADP). She has a second degree in Reiki and is certified by the Institute of Heart Math to teach Heart Coherence Techniques.

*She has hiked in the Andes, gone deep sea fishing in the Gulf of Mexico, been skydiving over the Hudson Valley, learned to scuba-dive on the Isle of Margarita in Venezuela, and has recently returned from a memory quest to Egypt. Contact Cydya at **www.cydyasmith.com.***

FREE GIFT

My Gift to You:

Learn the Heart of Stress Management

This concise training is filled with interesting data, questions and answers, and free resources.

For access, contact Cydya at **www.cydyasmith.com**

Chapter 6

Archaeology of My Soul

A Discovery of Divine Connectedness Over Time

By Jennifer Belanger

It was deep into the night, three days after my father's death. I was 11 years old and awoken out of a dead sleep to the presence of a shimmering, glowing resurrected cross floating at my bedside. I slowly sat up in my bed, wide-eyed and in awe, because right before me was the presence of my father as a resurrected cross. I somehow knew this instinctively; I was not afraid. I felt like time had stopped with this divine encounter as I connected with my dad like never before. I sat there in disbelief, taking it all in. A few moments later I laid back down and fell into a deep sleep.

I experienced the tragic loss of my father, James (Jim for short), the day after Christmas, 1980. So much had happened in such a short time—six months earlier, my father was diagnosed with cancer. He was a gentle soul—such a loving father—and very spiritual. My parents raised us Catholic and our family attended church every Sunday.

After painfully watching my father decline rapidly from cancer, his time came to leave this earth. My life suddenly changed drastically. With this tragic loss in our family, it was time to come into a place of existence without him; I was now fatherless. Not long after his passing, we sold our house and moved six hours away to another city. I had to leave behind everything I knew: my childhood home, some of my older siblings who decided to go on living in this city, my best friends, and my school. What I didn't leave behind were my memories of my dad; I brought those with me in my heart and into my new life.

There were two very special memories, along with the shimmering cross of my dad, that I brought with me into my new life, and they both have a spiritual connection. The first memory was about my dad telling me the story of Easter Sunday which links to my amazing supernatural cross encounter with my dad. It was bedtime on Holy Saturday; I was about eight years old and my dad was sitting at my bedside, describing the story of Easter Sunday to me where "the *big* boulder in front of Jesus' Tomb was rolled away; the tomb was empty because Jesus had Resurrected and He appeared to Mary Magdalene." I was listening so intensely as I loved this story. I could see the scene in my mind's eye as he described it, and felt what it would have been like to witness it. What is so astounding about this is that my dad was sitting in the exact location on my bed telling me about Jesus' Resurrection and, three years later, my dad appeared to me as a resurrected cross at the exact place at my bedside where he was telling me about Jesus' Resurrection on that Holy Saturday!

In more recent years, I have been thinking about these experiences with my dad and have shed light on so many parallels that relate to Jesus and Mary Magdalene. For example, I watched my dad suffer and slowly die as did Mary Magdalene watch Jesus suffer and slowly die. The emotionality in Mary Magdalene's heart watching her beloved suffer and slowly die is yet another mirror of my experience. My father died on a Friday, and Jesus died on Good Friday. We had our last supper with my dad on Thursday night and Jesus' Last Supper was on a Thursday night. It is interesting too with this timing as it was Jesus' birthday, Thursday December 25th, Christmas Day, when we had our last supper—yet another connection to Jesus here. Mark (15:33) reads that the world went dark at the sixth hour when Jesus was on the cross, and my world went dark at the end of six months when my father passed away. Jesus transitioned from His earthly body to His Resurrected body. He in a sense became the Resurrected Cross because Jesus was now off His Cross. Similarly, my dad went from his earthly body to his resurrected spirit when I witnessed him three days after his death in the form of a resurrected shimmering cross. Jesus transitioned to His Resurrected body and Mary Magdalene witnessed Him three days after His death. As you can see, witnessing my dad's resurrected cross at my bedside, in the *same* location where my dad told me about Jesus' Resurrection three years earlier, and Mary Magdalene's witness to Jesus' Resurrected body almost mirror each other. I felt emotions of disbelief and awe I would have to think Mary Magdalene felt when she saw Jesus, like me with my dad! It's so interesting because my Anthology chapter is being published the same month my supernatural experience with my dad occurred: December.

The second memory I brought with me into my new life had to do with a Volkswagen (VW) toy car my dad bought me at a store called Towers when I was seven years old. I had a big smile on my face when he bought me this toy car because, for some reason, when I was young, I loved VW cars. What is so amazing is that a VW car led me spiritually to Magdala, Israel—the home of Mary Magdalene. It's like my seven-year-old self instinctively knew on some level that a VW car/symbol would lead me to something so beautiful, which it did—Magdala! Years later, I noticed some very interesting parallels: the word Magdala in Jesus' spoken language, Aramaic, means "Tower," and the VW toy car was from "Towers." Also, Volkswagen is a German automobile and the city where my toy car was purchased was a German community. Moreover, it was a German scholar, Dr. Carl Reinhardt, who found Mary Magdalene's Gospel, which is known as the Berlin Codex, and the former name of the city where I got my toy car was once called Berlin! Overall, it's like my VW toy car connected me on some level to a real VW car, which in turn, led me to Magdala. Below I will take you on a ride to see how I was divinely guided to Magdala.

I was driving alone one morning, over ten years ago, thinking about some of the Gnostic gospels, including the *Gospel of Mary Magdalene,* as something had brought this to my attention days before. While I was driving (in my silver-colored vehicle), I came to a stop sign and in front of me was a silver Volkswagen Jetta (Jetta has the same number of characters as the name Jesus). I noticed a white Hawaiian lei hanging from the rearview mirror of the Jetta and the mirror represented the past. In that instant, I received information from the Holy Spirit. I was told there was something sacred hidden and it had to do with Hawaii. I immediately started thinking about what it could be and where that something was hidden in Hawaii.

At the same time, I could feel Jesus' presence with me in this mystical moment. I felt this was all related in some way to what I had been thinking about just moments before—the Gnostic gospels. There was a connection here. I was also shown about this place (where something sacred was hidden), in an almost humorous way, that I needed a "JET" "TA" (JETTA) to get there. My attention was brought to the song playing on the radio while my divine revelation was happening and the song was *Love Changes Everything* by a Canadian rock band called Honeymoon Suite. Some of the lyrics in this song really spoke to me, it was like Jesus speaking right to my heart. At the time, I was wearing a Celtic Cross on a string hanging down, right at my heart which related directly to some of the song lyrics. I gently touched my Cross and got the shivers because I realized the lyrics in this song were mirroring how my Cross was right at my heart. The lyrics in this song were perfectly timed for other parts of the Hawaii revelation.

Not long after I was shown this divine insight regarding Hawaii, I briefly overheard a news story on TV about an archaeological site where they discovered a synagogue in Israel, although I missed hearing where in Israel. I thought, wow, *isn't it interesting how recently I was shown that there is something sacred hidden somewhere in Hawaii and there is this sacred discovery in Israel which made me think of Jesus.* For some reason, I never looked into that synagogue news story any further and actually forgot about it. The VW Jetta car experience was the beginning of a revelation that was to unfold more in God's timing right up until 2013 and onwards.

In 2013 I started teacher's college at the age of 44. Within a month of being in school, my anxiety got so intense I had to leave the program. My whole world crashed and shifted in trying so desperately to find myself—I thought this was my career path: I would be working with children, and would have a well-paying job, benefits, and would fit in with society's ways with a career like this. I had it all figured out, or so I thought. With this huge and unexpected shift, I suddenly felt so very lost and distraught. I couldn't understand what had happened. My world had fallen apart, my nervous system was in overdrive and I began therapy. I had never felt so overtaken by my anxiety and there didn't seem to be anything that could help me so I cried out to God from the depths of my soul and asked Him to heal me and please tell me what this was all about. I began to get even more serious about my faith and my relationship to God, Jesus, and the Holy Spirit and opened my heart more. I joined Bible study groups, listened to preachers, read religious books and spent a lot of time in prayer. Through this journey of faith and my deep connection with God, I began to feel more whole and became more spiritually awakened. As this took place, more and more revelations opened up to me about what mirrors there were in my life to Jesus, Mary Magdalene, and the Holy Land. I felt the Lord say to me that He wanted me to write the story He created in me, this story—Archaeology of My Soul. That is part of my purpose: to write my story and grow in knowing God at a deeper level. Teacher's college was not the way, as I was painfully shown. My soul knew this was not the route and it responded with intense anxiety to guide me in a new direction.

Ironically, it was the wrong turn to teacher's college that brought me closer to God, so in fact, it really wasn't a wrong turn. The incredible thing is that I did get something so profound out of briefly going to teacher's college. While I was still enrolled in this program, I was looking at possibly teaching abroad temporarily in Israel because I have a deep passion for the Holy Land; the place my Savior Jesus lived and walked.

On my mother's birthday in August of 2013, I began looking online at the Israeli Department of Education in Jerusalem to see if they offered any temporary teaching opportunities for teachers from other countries and didn't really find anything. I was just about to shut down my computer for the night, but then felt called to look at a map of Jerusalem. I scrolled around, looking at various places and street names. I began to think how surprised I was that I had never thought of doing this before—taking a virtual tour of Israel—since I had never been there. Although it was getting late, I felt this nudge to continue looking at this map. I could feel the Holy Spirit guiding me north on the map of Israel. I saw the Dead Sea and continued heading north to Galilee. I thought, *Galilee is where Jesus performed many of His miracles and ministered to the people.* How excited I felt. It was in that moment that a word jumped off the page for me along the northwest shore of Galilee—it was the word "Hawaii"—the Hawaii Beach Resort—and it was in Magdala. In an instant, I heard the Holy Spirit say to me that *this* was the Hawaii location from my past revelation and *not* Hawaii, USA, as I had originally thought. I was wide-eyed and had the shivers as I had just learned that this was the place where something sacred was located; Hawaii Beach Resort at Magdala, Galilee. I had tears in my eyes as I was shown a big piece of this sacred puzzle. At that moment, I had no idea that the first-century synagogue was already discovered at this exact site in 2009. Why the time delay, I do not know. This was done in God's perfect timing, to serve His purpose. This first-century synagogue was where Jesus taught, scholars believe, and, in my heart, I believe this too.

Back in 2013, I told my husband about this additional revelation and said that I would love to go to Magdala's Hawaii Beach Resort and start digging because I know there was something sacred hidden there. I told him this over a latte at Starbucks. I said, "There is something big there," again, not knowing yet about the 2009 first-century Magdala synagogue discovery along with the ruins of ancient Magdala—the home of Mary Magdalene. However, I didn't follow through on this revelation as I thought people would think it was ridiculous of me to want to go to this Magdala site and start digging for something, so I let it go. About a year later I was guided to an article about the 2009 Magdala synagogue discovery; I couldn't believe my eyes, there was something hidden there, this solidified my knowing that something sacred was there— the first-century synagogue and ancient Magdala!

In 2019, my husband and I traveled to the Holy Land and visited Magdala. It was the most incredible feeling to be there; my vision and spiritual download of this place years earlier came into reality. I was so grateful to Jesus who led me there, spiritually first, then, years later, physically.

My childhood memories, as I have discovered decades later, play an important part in my story and are so inter-woven. I would have never thought that all of these experiences I had would lead me to the Holy Land. I have witnessed how intricate God is and how He connects people, places and things in such an incredible way. All of these profound, divinely orchestrated events, and synchronicities give you an idea of what I have experienced over the years.

I will be writing more about my divine experiences and visions in my book that I am working on, *Archaeology of My Soul* (the title of my chapter is taken from my book title). It is in my quiet moments, when I am connecting with God, is when I receive insights, revelations and visions. It is also within my sacred breath that I breathe that connects me deeply with God. Yahweh is another word for God and when I inhale this sacred word and exhale, it brings me to even deeper levels of connection with Him. "Yahweh breathed His name over humanity, bringing us to life," as stated in the documentary *Breath of Life* by Daniel Kooman. This word for God is powerfully used with the breath because God breathed life into us through our nostrils. In Genesis (2:7) it says, "The Lord God (Yahweh) formed man of the dust of the ground and breathed into his nostrils the breath of life and man became a living soul." We can see how powerful the breath is—it is a gift from our Creator.

I have so much passion for the sacred breath that I have recently become a Certified Breathwork Facilitator. I help people connect with their bodies, emotions, and to our Divine Creator within us—God. Also, my 2013 turning point story eventually led me to breathwork so I could grow even more in my spiritual life and heal myself.

Use your breath to awaken to the subtle clues and follow your spiritual bread crumbs. Have you been alert to your spiritual bread crumbs, and if so, what are they telling you? Does your childhood have something to reveal to you with your life's purpose? I encourage you to connect with your sacred breath and the archaeology of your soul.

My experiences that I have shared with you were the beginning of a sacred puzzle with a spiritual theme within it. As ancient Magdala was being uncovered at this archaeological site, so too was I uncovering a metaphorical archaeological site within me. I am so grateful to be given the spiritual eyes to see and ears to hear what God has shown me from the past to today.

Finally, my chapter in this anthology has been published by Flower of Life Press—and their company logo is the Flower of Life symbol. Interestingly enough, Magdala's logo, taken from the Magdala Stone in the first-century synagogue looks very similar to the Flower of Life. What an amazing connection of sacred geometry in my story with Flower of Life Press and Magdala.

As I breathe and go within, I observe with awe and curiosity, God's ways of connecting so many entities in my life over time to Jesus, Mary Magdalene, and the Holy Land. You, too, have treasure within you because the Creator of the Universe lives inside of you.

"When I met Jennifer and her husband in June of 2019 to visit Magdalene's grotto, she told me that she had been to Magdala and that her experience had been extraordinary. I would never have thought of the paths she took to get to this place where Myrhiam and Jeshua lived and taught. Her experience is overwhelming. She recounts her journey with great love and is not afraid to open her heart. I admire her writing for different reasons: her way of writing, her honesty and her determination, but also her fragility. She brilliantly shows that by opening a door, other doors open and lead us to Revelation, capital R. Revelation of our life mission, Revelation of the Divine within us to lead us ever closer to God."

—Veronique Flayol, French lecturer specializing in pilgrimages and spiritual journeys on Mary Magdalene's footsteps

FREE GIFT

A Breathwork Gift for You! Receive free access to **a breathwork audio recording** on my website where, as a certified Breathwork Facilitator, I talk about the sacred breath and how it connects you to your inner wisdom. I guide you through a short breathwork meditation to help you connect to your inner wisdom.

I would also like to offer you a **30-minute virtual breathwork session** at a one-time discounted price of 30% off (offer good until January 31, 2024.)

Please visit **www.jenniferbelanger.com/special-gift** to access the audio recording and/or schedule a 30-minute breathwork session over Zoom. Be sure to use the PROMO CODE: **TURNING-POINTSTORIES** for the 30% off discount.

I look forward to meeting you!

JENNIFER BELANGER *is a spiritual person who has uncovered treasure within herself through her connection to God. She has over a decade of mystical experiences, visions, and revelations which have led her to write her story. The profound revelations from God and how He has inter-woven His mysteries through Jennifer will ignite your own soul as you will see God's divinity within her chapter and will witness more once her book* Archaeology of My Soul *is complete. Her prayer life and desire to understand God's Word has brought her to studying scripture. In 2019, Jennifer traveled to the Holy Land on a spiritual pilgrimage and witnessed all of the sacred places that God showed her in her revelations and visions.*

Jennifer lives in Canada and loves to spend time outdoors, hiking, biking, and camping with her husband and children. Jennifer is a Breathwork Facilitator and connects people with their sacred breath to help them find their own archaeological treasure within.

Visit Jennifer's Website: **www.jenniferbelanger.com**

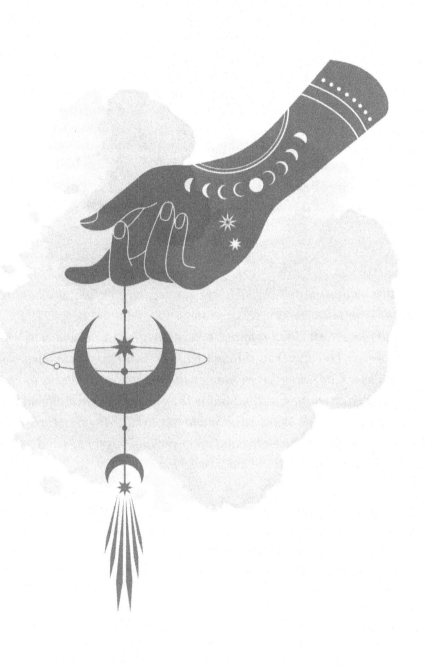

Chapter 7

On the Path of Angels

By Marial Dreamwalker

My body froze as I felt the cold steel barrel under my chin. I turned my face away from him to avoid the stench of stale whiskey and cigarettes on his breath. He ran the barrel down the front of my body, stopping just below my navel, where he pressed the barrel into my flesh.

"I should just shoot you here since your uterus is no good anyway. What good are you? You can't even give me a baby, you're useless."

I married Joseph to escape the control of several family members who sexually abused me from the age of four to the age of twelve. Even though I left home at seventeen, had a full-time job and my own flat, my abusers still tried to control aspects of my life. I often dreamed of a man who was strong and powerful. Someone who could protect me and was not intimidated by the males in my family. Joseph was a martial artist. He was tall and strong and had a resemblance to Sylvester Stallone. Yet in that moment, I felt he was right. I couldn't have a baby. We had been together for six years and I'd had three miscarriages.

I loved children and I wanted a baby more than anything. Becoming a mother was an expectation and rite of passage for a Mexican woman. Each of my siblings already had several children. I felt betrayed by my body. I loved my nieces and nephews, but I ached for a child of my own. I was twenty-six years old, and felt that as a woman, I was a failure. Joseph got violent and verbally abusive whenever he drank, which, after I miscarried, became a nightly ritual. I thought about what my own mother had said to me when I tried to leave Joseph once before and asked to stay with her.

"You wanted to be married? Well this is what marriage is like. Go home to your husband."

That night, I went to Ocean Beach instead. I had several valiums and a bottle of Vodka in hand. I was at the end of a very thin rope. I knew if I didn't leave, he would kill me. I screamed prayers of rage and grief to the sea, to the Goddess, and to whomever else was listening.

"You find me a way out of this, or I'm going to end this torture that my life. I don't want this life anymore. I need a way out. Help me, please."

I swallowed the valium with the vodka and cried until I had no more tears, then passed out on the sand. When I woke up the next morning, I was angry to discover I was still alive. I couldn't go home, so I took the bus to Gifts of the Goddess bookstore in the Mission to visit Sally, who was my friend and the owner. This store was my sanctuary. I usually went there on Saturdays when they offered psychic readings. But I was content to quietly browse the bookshelves, a cup of tea in hand, and allow the healing energy from the crystals and herbs to permeate my mind and body. For those few hours, I felt at peace.

That morning, I stumbled into the bookstore hungover, with sand in my hair. Sally rushed over to give me a hug and marched me to the bathroom in the back of the store so I could brush the sand out of my hair and splash water on my face. When I came out of the bathroom, she was waiting with a hot cup of tea.

"Are you okay, Mari? I'm worried about you; you look terrible. You know I don't like to tell people what to do, but I think you really should get a reading. Juana is here today, and she has advised me through some tough times. I trust her."

Before I could answer, Sally waved Juana over to the counter where she introduced us. Juana put her arm around my shoulder and guided me over to a small square table in the corner of the store. When we sat down, she took my left hand and placed it on the table palm up. She reached into a small leather bag around her neck and took out Mugwort. She pinched them between her fingers, sprinkling it into my hand. Then she looked deep into my eyes. I felt as if she could see into me, and suddenly I could see her more clearly, too. She had a violet aura, a spattering of freckles across her nose, and a compassionate smile. But it was her eyes that drew me in. They were a clear cerulean blue, elongated like cats' eyes. I felt a fire from her, yet she emanated love and compassion. Her words carried a weight of intensity and urgency.

"You are a born healer and a vessel for divine transmission. I see that you have received these visitations from the angels since before you could speak. I know you can see and hear spirits, even though you don't talk about it. You have angels and guides around you who are protecting you. But even so, you are in great danger. The angels can help you only so much. You need to listen to your heart and follow where you are guided. You must leave San Francisco as soon as possible. There will be someone who will appear in your life very soon who will help you. If you don't leave, your husband is going to kill you. It is time to take your life in your own hands and change your destiny. Are you ready?"

I couldn't have been more ready. I knew my prayers were being answered.

"Yes. I'm ready. I will follow your advice. Thank you, Juana."

"Good. On your way out, pick up a copy of *Common Ground* magazine. There is an ad for a psychic development class in the back pages. You don't need it, but you should sign up for it. Remember, when flowers are ready, nothing can stop them from blooming."

I can't explain it, but I knew I could trust Juana. I did as she instructed and when I got home, I flipped through the magazine to find the ad she spoke about. I found the ad; *Unfold and Bloom in Beauty*. I immediately signed up for the class. Over the six weeks I went to see Juana and each time she advised me how to protect myself from Joseph's negative intentions. She also told me about Reiki healing energy and how it would help me ground my gifts as a healer. After that I started seeing flyers for Reiki classes everywhere I went. I had never heard of it before, and I really could not afford to pay for another class at that time. I kept Juana's words close to me. I knew that if it was meant to happen, Reiki would find me.

On the last night of the psychic development class, one of the women named Lora approached me. She was an older woman with wise eyes that told me she had also been through a lot in her life.

"You seem like you are going through a rough time, Mari. I can feel that you're in danger. You don't have to go through this alone. Believe me, I have been where you are, and I know how scary it can be."

I hadn't said anything to Lora, but after all, this was a class for psychics. When she spoke, my heart expanded, and I knew I was being guided. After I told her about my abuse, she took my hand.

"You are coming home with me tonight and tomorrow I'll take you back to get your things. You can stay with me for as long as you need to."

I went home with Lora that night and the next day she drove me back to my apartment where we loaded up my belongings in her truck. I left San Francisco to begin my new life. I moved only forty minutes to the city of Martinez, but no one knew where I was, and for the first time in years, I was free.

A few weeks later, I took the BART into San Francisco. I wanted to see Juana again and tell her everything that had happened. When I got to the bookstore, Sally was happy to see me.

"Mari! Where have you been? I haven't seen you for weeks." She gave me a hug.

"I came to see Juana. I have so much to tell her. What time will she be in today?"

Sally furrowed her brow. "Juana? Who are you talking about?" At first, I thought she was joking, but then I realized she was serious, and I started to panic.

"Sally, I had four readings with her over the last few months. She has blue eyes, and she reads with herbs. You were the one who introduced us and told me to get a reading with her in the first place. We sat right over there." I pointed to the table in the corner where we sat each Saturday. I felt like I was in an episode of Twilight Zone.

"I'm sorry Mari, I don't know who you are talking about. Look, you're my friend and I care about you, but there has never been a reader named Juana here. That table is where Marta reads tarot. Are you sure you didn't go to another store for a reading?"

"There isn't any other store, Sally. This is the only place I come on Saturdays. You know that."

I tried not to raise my voice as the panic began to rise. I was confused and scared. I didn't understand what was happening and didn't know what to do about it. Suddenly, I couldn't breathe, and I had to get out of there. Sally didn't understand what was going on with me, and to be honest, I was beginning to doubt all of it. Then, as I was leaving the store, I glanced over to the magazine stand and noticed the cover of the latest *Common Ground*. It had a photograph of hands surrounded by light. The heading read, *Reiki Classes: Your Guide to Training in the Bay Area.* I let out a big sigh as I remembered Juana's words. I knew in my heart she was real, even if I had no tangible proof. I caught the train back to Martinez, still feeling a bit confused. Did I imagine Juana? Yet everything she said had guided me to safety. As the train pulled into the station, I said a prayer.

"Juana, if you are real, please give me proof, so I know I didn't imagine this." Later that week, I wandered into a metaphysical store and decided to ask if they were hiring. They had a part-time retail position available, so I took an application and returned it the next day. The owner of the store happened to be working behind the counter. I gave her my application and she hired me on the spot. As she told me about the bookstore, she mentioned that they offered Reiki classes. Just then, Carol, the Reiki Master Teacher, walked into the store. The owner, Lilia, introduced us. Carol looked at me and said,

"Oh, good, I'm going to be traveling to China and You're going to be the new Reiki Master Teacher here." I was stunned with joy. Reiki had found me! Lilia listened carefully to what Carol was saying. She must have felt it was meant to be because she gifted me with the Reiki attunements necessary to become the new Reiki instructor for the store. I was elated. I knew I was in the right place and that my new life was beginning right in front of me, just as Juana had said.

A week later, I had my first Reiki attunement. Carol stood in front of a chair in the room. Soft music was playing, white candles were lit, and the fragrance of sage smoke filled the air. Carol motioned for me to sit in the chair. I removed my shoes and jewelry and sat down. She said a prayer to invite my guides and angels and offered gratitude to the Reiki ancestors. Then she walked behind me and placed her hands on top of my head. I felt a gentle heat move from her hands through my entire body. When Carol completed my Reiki attunement, she stepped out of the room to give me time to process my attunement.

When I opened my eyes, there was a large being of light floating in front of me; it felt feminine. She vibrated violet, pink, emerald, and golden light that pulsed and resonated through me. Then she sang a song made of light that moved through me like a cleansing river. Then, I saw tremendous white wings appear and enfolded me in her love. It was pure, vast, and completely unconditional. She pulled me into her, and as I gazed more closely, I saw elongated cerulean eyes, faceted like a gemstone.

"Who are you?" I asked.

"I am Sharova of the Crystalline Devas of the Rose Ray. Welcome home, Mari. You have found your path. You are a healer of light, frequency, and vibration from the celestial realms. She began to hum, and her wings swirled around me. Suddenly, I felt like I was choking—an ocean of tears caught in my throat. Then I remembered when I was four years old, I started to receive visitations from orbs of light. They would sing to me and envelop me with their love. This occurred during a time when I was being sexually and physically abused by adults in my family.

"We have been waiting for you to remember us, Mari." When I heard her voice, the ocean of tears I had been holding came pouring through. Having been treated like garbage for most of my life, which was how I felt—dirty, useless, unwanted, full of secrets and shame. When my tears finally subsided, I was left with a clarity of identity apart from all the abuse I had suffered, along with a sense of deep belonging with these divine beings. I had a sense of worthiness and purpose I had never felt before.

"Yes, I remember you. I have missed you and I didn't even realize it. Still, I don't understand why I had to suffer like this."

"Soon you will understand, my beloved, and soon you will understand the gifts you possess. Gifts that are to be shared with others who have gone through similar sorrows. Now that you are able to hear us again, you will be able to consciously receive our guidance and assistance. You are free. We want you to know that we cherish you with a love that is beyond your human understanding. Your heart is the key to experiencing this love and will allow you to access your divine nature."

"But how will I be sure it's you?"

"Your courage and trust are what brought you here, beloved. We have been with you since before you incarnated on this earth. You are a part of us, and although you may not understand it now, you came to the earth for a specific mission. One that your essence chose." Suddenly the image of Juana and her cerulean blue eyes appeared in my mind, and I understood why Sally did not remember Juana. My encounter with her happened in the angelic realm.

The Reiki attunement I received was a vehicle that cleared my energy bodies and healing channels, so I was able to see and hear my guides as I did when I was a child. I felt a renewed joy and childlike wonder in my heart. Over the next two months, I completed my Reiki training and became the Reiki Master Teacher at the Infinity Bookstore. This was the beginning of my healing journey. I began to remember the sexual abuse I had blocked out with alcohol. It was devastating, and at the same time, I felt reborn. I still had a long journey ahead of me, and there were times I didn't want to remember anymore. It was too painful, but Sharova kept her promise. She was there with me every step of the way. She guided me and comforted me. She was also with me when I performed energy healings for others. She guided my hands and eyes to understand the underlying issues the person was experiencing. People often reported feeling an angelic presence around me.

"That's Sharova." I took that opportunity to introduce them to the *Divas*, as I lovingly refer to them.

It has been three decades since that time in my life. A large part of the work I do with others involves helping them to establish a relationship with the angelic realm. I specialize in collaborating with women survivors of trauma. My own trauma unfolded into a path of beauty and service to others. Sharing what I have learned about energy, angels, and healing allows me to help women to uncover the gifts that hide within the trauma.

MARIAL DREAMWALKER *is a fourth generation Xicana Energy Medicine Carrier. She holds a BA in Chicana Studies, an MA in Women's Spirituality, and an MFA in Creative Nonfiction Writing from New College of California, where she taught spiritual autobiography and energy healing. She grew up in the Mission District of San Francisco, immersed in Indigenous culture, sacred ritual, and art. She is a Reiki Maestra, artist, writer, singer-songwriter, and an international channel for the divine feminine and the angelic realm. Marial was first visited by the Goddesses Tonanzin-Guadalupe, La Llorona, Mother Mary, along with the Archangels Michael and the Crystalline Devas of the Rose Ray during times she experienced severe sexual childhood trauma.*

Marial has been a member of the Healing Clinic Collective in Oakland, CA for over ten years, which brings alternative healing services to low-income communities at no cost. Marial is an initiator and spiritual catalyst who guides women through the darkness of trauma to bring awareness of the strengths and gifts from within their wounding. The Teachings of the Sacred Shawl were given to Marial by the goddesses La Llorona and Tonantzin-Guadalupe. She integrates these indigenous teachings with sacred ceremony, writing and creativity to help women heal their hearts and understand their innate empathic and healing gifts.

Marial also utilizes sound healing to activate cellular memory to align you with your soul purpose. Her current heart-vision is to create an online sacred temple for women from all over the world to learn the Teachings of the Sacred Shawl, create a global network that serves to bring women into alignment with their soul purpose. Her work also serves to dismantle the colonized demonization of La Llorona and to elevate her to her rightful place as an Indigenous goddess of the Americas.

Marial is a Flower of Life Press author and is currently finishing her forthcoming novel, Keeper of The Sacred Shawl, *which will be published in 2023. You can read more of Marial's writing and learn more about her classes and workshops at **www.maridreamwalker.com** to sign up for her blog and receive a special gift. You can also listen to her music at **www.reverbnation.com/maridreamwalker.***

FREE GIFT

My Gifts to You:

Angelic Alignment Transmission—A complimentary angelic alignment transmission.

Also, read **a chapter from my upcoming novel, *The Keeper of the Sacred Shawl,*** and learn the truth about the creation of La Llorona: Goddess of Sacred Tears.

To access, visit **www.maridreamwaker.com/gift**

CHAPTER 8

Believe Someone's Listening

By Caryl Anne Engel

You may be wondering why I'm here. No, I don't mean here on *Planet Earth—that's* another story for a different time. I mean, here, in this book: how I got to be a first-time published author. Being a writer has been my dream for twenty years and I've had a pen and piece of paper in my hand since I was eleven years old. I promised God that I would share my story with the world if I could be healed from the early circumstances in my life that had impacted me deeply.

I've been on a lot of pharmaceuticals since I was twenty-five years old, and I can't tell you all their names…but I can say for a time, I was wildly devoted to Xanax. Things are better now, and I am keeping my promise to write a spiritual memoir about my healing process. It's my dream to share my story and help others. Things weren't always as they are now, with synchronicities, gifts, and opportunities falling into my lap. Not. At. All. It seems that when I finally discovered my path—*my path*…the one my Soul had agreed to before I came in—Spirit did a U-turn, pulled a solid, and made things move forward.

I feel myself awakening. The previous ten years, it was one step forward and two (okay, three, sometimes five) steps back; that dance. My life changed in an instant three years ago, literally from a miracle born out of a prayer to my Divine Feminine guide, Mary Magdalene. Yet, it was a long journey there and I want to share some of it with you. Please stay until the end; it really gets better! It makes me happy to give you hope.

So much to share in this short space. First, I will tell you how Mary Magdalene found me. It was in 2010, in an art room. My sister and I had gone to Bishop's Ranch Episcopalian Retreat Center in Alexander Valley of Northern California for an Advent retreat. It was a silent retreat for three full days. The only sounds allowed were chanting, singing, and chewing. When not engaged in these activities, we lounged in the manor house by the enormous stone fireplace in communal meditation. Being with kindred souls without actually having to talk? Delicious. After the first day, I discovered there was an art room in the basement of the chapel. There we found images of saints in a paper box with small pieces of rectangular wood. We could make icons. There was Mother Mary, Hildegarde, and a lovely woman with a long red braid.

"Who is this?" I whispered to the woman beside me, breaking the rules.

"Mary Magdalene," she whispered back.

Huh. In my Episcopalian upbringing, I had always been drawn to Mary Magdalene; the "penitent prostitute" who anointed Jesus' feet with oil. She appeared annually for our church's Passion Play before Easter and then disappeared until the following Lent. Strangely, I always felt connected to her. Somehow, I understood her suffering. I sensed a mysterious, deep love she seemed to have for Jesus, and which He also seemed to have for her. During the Passion Play, I longed to go up on the altar and hold her, to put my face in her long, red hair.

In the art room, I pasted her image on rectangular wood, then hammered tiny little silver nails into the metal trim, and painted colorful designs around her. I continued to make icons of her. Eventually, my sister wondered why I wasn't showing up at Chapel.

"Do I need to be *worried* about you?" she asked one evening in our room, in a big sisterly way.

"I'm fine. I'm enjoying painting icons of Mary Magdalene."

At home, she sat on my shelf. I somewhat forgot about her. A few years later, she would make an exuberant reappearance in my life, and this time she stayed. More on that later.

Before that time, I was the flower crouching at the back of the garden. Afraid of the light, I was scared of how bright I might bloom. My voice could get me in trouble. Exposure, telling my story—it came with risks. I worried I wasn't strong enough, yet alternately feared I was *too* powerful. Earlier life events had held me hostage to my own limiting beliefs. They included: *Things always mess up. The common denominator in this is me. Life can't be trusted. I'm not worthy. Who am I to? Maybe I'm just not that special.* It took years of healing to clear my wounded mantras. Until then, I lingered in the shadows, preferring shade and cloud cover to the sunny, bright light of Northern California where I ended up in my thirties.

I left Ohio in 1989, where I had a professional planning job after college. For one, it was the scene of an early crime that followed me like an anxious, smelly dog. Plus, the Midwest had begun to feel stifling. I sensed a call to begin my spiritual journey, though I had absolutely no idea what that meant. Also, I had family in California.

I loaded my Pontiac Ventura to the gills (my friend Lisa called it "The Leisure Suit" due to its 1970s brown and tan plaid interior) and upon arrival, began to explore the vast array of New Age delights that California offered. At first, I was like a child ogling weird, spiky fish at the Chinese Restaurant aquarium. Then, I dipped my finger, then toe in…Before long I dove head-long and swam around with them. Look at my crazy red stripes! Aren't my electric blue fins fantastic? *Bloopety-bloop-bloop.*

However, having been a professional in my twenties, I still felt the need to *look* respectable on the outside. I went to graduate school for Counseling Psychology (check!) plowed through 3000 endless intern hours (check, groan), treated traumatized souls in my office, which, as an Empath, got my nervous system all jangly (uncheck), began my licensure as a Marriage and Family Therapist, (check) and then…Spirit swooped in and chided me for not heeding warnings that this wasn't the right career path due to my sensitive and spiritual nature, and kiboshed my licensing process in a most dramatic manner; over a technicality (double—uncheck!) My graduate school friends' faces visibly winced when they heard my story. Yet, the night it happened, I got drunk and danced around the living room. I was free!

During those intern years I made $7.00/hour and needed to supplement my income at random hours. Northern California's Wine Country was beautiful, but its agricultural economy did not offer many options other than tourism and hospitality, and no one seemed impressed with my counseling masters (sigh). A friend suggested I look into "on-call nannying." On nights and weekends, I began caring for children at hotels whose parents were on vacation or attending business functions. I enjoyed the children and they me, with my Mary Poppins bag full of toys. Plus, I got room service in a luxurious hotel room after I put the kids to bed. My niche soon became infants and babies. I found they delighted me—mostly—except when they screamed on and on for so long, I wondered why they didn't literally stroke out, and would I need to call 911? I learned that tiny humans are born with extremely strong wills and when angry, will endeavor to cause all manner of suffering in their caregiver. This includes panic, sweating, praying, dread, helplessness, more sweating, and crying to God to make the crying stop. I had to figure something out, fast! Through my power of intuition (i.e., begging angels for help) I became a Baby Whisperer. I could win over a six-month-old who was leaving mommy for the first time in a strange hotel room, and with baby jet lag (checkity-check!)

During the 2008 recession however, the tourist industry waned, and I began working with families on a permanent basis. There I learned: surprise! Babies grow to toddlers and toddlers go to preschool, where they carry home a never-ending supply of contagious, radioactive snot. As kids developed their immune system, mine was tanking. They sneezed in my face. I held them when they were feverish. I was sick all the time. I worked doing shots of Theraflu and espresso. Most troubling, I discovered two-year-olds are *actually easier* than three-year-olds, whose still reptilian emotions are now encased in the entitled belief that at three, they know *everything*, and you, in turn, are a complete imbecile. Do not (ever!) tell a three-year-old little girl what to wear to preschool, or you will have to go stab yourself with a kitchen knife. One time, I actually worried the neighbors would call the police.

Finally, due to weeks-long flus and a sore back from picking up babies off the floor twenty times a day, I resigned myself to the fact that my days of soothing little babies to sleep were over. I retired my Baby Whisperer hat and threw it in the landfill with the 10,000 soiled Pampers I had changed over the years.

Also—then I had to have brain surgery. After breaking up with my boy-friend in what can only be described as a "How the f—k did I not know this?" manner, I had a CAT scan. The neurosurgeon said, "See that boulder on the screen? That's a tumor crushing your pituitary. Thankfully, it's not cancerous, but it's coming out right away, or you'll lose your eyesight."

I had lost contact with the man who had been my most supportive friend (he had a Very! New! Girlfriend!) and went under the knife in an eight-hour surgery. The neurosurgeon assured me this was, "routine brain surgery" and that "really, you'll be fine! And soon!" A little-known fact is that in the history of surgery, *no* surgeons have ever actually *had surgery* (this was confirmed by six other people I knew who'd also had surgery.) They vastly under-estimate recovery time. The promised six weeks turned into eight months. I went into debt, and needed to find employment…but where? I had to find a job with folks who had my energy level…*I know! Old people!* I worked with elders who had Alzheimer's, heart disease, diabetes, stroke, and general Very Old Age. I also cared for my mom during those years, who was declining from Vascular Dementia. Except for the time a client with Parkinson's dementia dashed off to the bathroom on his walker, pulling his pants down on the way, with me lurching forward to catch the, yes—steam-ing poop in my bare hand—I mostly enjoyed my clients. *This will be me some day,* I told myself. *I'm paying it forward to my own decrepitude.* Elders wanted companionship, laughs, a nice drive on a sunny day, pretending you've heard their great story for the first time, home cooking, and help going to the bathroom—which, turns out, is many, *many* times a day. They also need a loving, calm presence as they pass on to the next realm. I found I was built to offer these services.

During this time, I certified as a *Divine Lens Soul Coach* and started a business called *Angel Speak.* I am clairaudient (I hear guidance) and offer intuitive readings while speaking to my clients' angels. Sometimes loved ones from the Other Side pop in. My guides clapped, exclaiming *Now you're listening, girl!* Respectability returned. Look at me, I have a nice office with my name on the door! Years passed…

…then, COVID hit. My clients went into hiding along with the rest of the world, in that alarmed state resembling a meltdown and a coma. I had my daily walks in my country neighborhood. A friend had blessedly moved in next door three days before lockdown. We shouted over the fence "Do you have any mayonnaise?"

Aside from the obvious, 2020 was challenging. A client moved overnight, leaving me jobless. I found a new client (eventually) yet, we had our challenges. I started on the very day Joe Biden won Pennsylvania (we won't talk politics here. I love all people, et cetera, et cetera) but she had pictures of herself with Ronald Reagan around the house. She seemed quite upset about the state of affairs. There were outbursts, accusations and glares as the Wall Street Journal landed on the breakfast table in the morning. I danced masterfully, with general positive aphorisms like, "I'm sure we all can agree on…"

I liked her cat.

What am I doing with my life? I thought. *Where has my life purpose gone?* A gray, flat cloud followed me through my day. This is probably a good time to tell you about how Mary Magdalene re-emerged in my life. I had begun working on my memoir and a member of my writing group ran upstairs one day and breathlessly came down waving a book called *The Expected One*, by Kathleen McGowan. "You've GOT to read this!" she said. "It's about Mary Magdalene!"

I was living with my boyfriend at the time, and though I felt our relationship drifting away like fog, a quiet fire crackled inside while reading her books. Mary Magdalene became my red-haired, red-robed friend. She comforted me, saying, "We're sisters, you know? I am strong. Lean on me. I will help you find your path again." A growing global sisterhood seemed to simultaneously be discovering the same.

Mary Magdalene was not a penitent prostitute. That sh*t was made up. She was a towering, spiritually powerful woman who landed in Southwest France after Jesus' crucifixion. She evangelized it in the *Way of Love*: Jesus' pure teachings of Gnosis, finding God inside one's self and equality between men and women. The Cathar culture evolved from these roots. For over a thousand years, the Cathar version of Christianity thrived in this area, embodying the teaching's simple, egalitarian principles. That is, until they were systematically eradicated during Europe's first horrific genocide, spawned by the Roman Catholic Church and the Inquisition. In 1969, the Vatican recanted the prostitute version of Mary Magdalene, yet such a tiny footnote over centuries of lies hardly made a dent; until a few, pioneering researchers and writers, such as Kathleen McGowan and Margaret Starbird, began to set the record straight. Pope Francis has recently called Mary Magdalene, "Our new and greatest hope" and considers her, "the Apostle of the Apostles."

Then, I learned that Kathleen McGowan led tours to "Sacred France," where her book, *The Expected One*, took place. Shazam! *I had to go!* My ancient genes called out: *You must go walk with Mary Magdalene on her home turf. You must—you WILL take this trip.*

My partner and I broke up, and during this time, Mary Magdalene and the books I read about her sustained me. They were a touchstone, a promise. Fast forward through heartbreak, brain surgery, the sore back, screaming babies, the pooping elders, and now, a client I tiptoed around, trying to keep the conversation, as my mother would say, "pleasant!"

One morning, I got an email in my inbox: Kathleen McGowan's *Secrets of the Cathars and Mysteries of the Magdalene Tour* in France was filling up. There were only two more spots. A deposit was required by the following Monday. It's now Winter 2020, and I was in my doldrums. All I wanted was to attend the Sacred France tour. My heart—no, my *Soul*, felt called. But how? Each step on that morning's walk was a prayer to Mary Magdalene. I told her, *I need a miracle. The trip is closing. I don't even have the deposit.* I walked back, head lowered, saying to myself, I guess I'll have to go next year. Always next year. What miracle could produce the funds for a trip so out of my financial range?

Two days later, my friend Wendy called. She is literally my oldest friend. Our parents went to college together and raised their families in Cleveland. Her mom, Davy, and mine, Peggy, introduced their wiggling babies Wendy and Caryl, and we've been friends ever since. Wendy later moved to California as I did, and every six months or so, we'd meet up at Half Moon Bay to catch up. COVID kiboshed that and it had been two years.

Wendy said, "We need to get together! Can you meet this Friday?"

"Yes, I'm free Friday!" I exclaimed.

Our schedules always required at least a month or two to plan a get-to-gether. But this time, it was so *easy*. We walked on the beach and were awed by the ocean's huge, dramatic waves that day. I described my bitter client, and lamented the general atmosphere of edgy discord that the whole world seemed to be feeling. I'm sure she noticed the hovering gray cloud above my head…and then told her I needed to get back on the road to beat Friday traffic.

She said, "No! You're not leaving yet. 2020 has been dreadful; we must share our positive dreams and intentions for 2021." She told me hers. Then she asked, "What's yours?" I paused and sighed inwardly. What's the point of bringing up something that won't happen? In my best Eeyore voice, I said, "Well, there's this trip to France." I told her about *The Expected One*, about my guide Mary Magdalene, and the Ancient Cathars. "It's not going to happen, Wendy. I can't make the deposit deadline. The trip is filling up. Next Monday it closes." I told her it was okay; I'd go next year and started to walk down the sandy path edged with sea grass toward my car.

Wendy said: "STOP. You're not getting in that car yet. You're going on the trip! *Davy's* taking you!" I looked at her. "What…what do you mean?" Davy had passed away three years prior from Alzheimer's. "That's impossible, Wendy!" I protested, confused. "Your mom was in a care facility for years…you can't possibly have been left with funds." She looked straight into my face in that earnest way and said, "No. We were. You know my mom's passion for world travel and following birds around the planet… nothing would make her happier than to help you go on this trip. It's settled! SHE'S TAKING YOU." Then she backtracked and said, "Oh, wait! I should not presume you are comfortable with this. Please take your time to think about it. I don't want to be patroniz-…"

"I accept! Okay!" I blurted, and we burst out laughing. Something surreal…magical had surely just happened. I don't remember the trip home, except having the vague sense that my life had just changed. Two days later, a check for the full amount was in my mailbox. I secured my place on the trip.

Turning point. Prayer answered, miracle delivered: the timing of Wendy's call, the unlikely easy scheduling of our get-together, her insistence that we talk about 2021. Six months later, I was on a plane to France. It was the first time I had traveled abroad in over twenty years. And I must tell you, I've not been the same since—in a good way. Sacred France, the Occitaine region…visiting ancient sites I knew I'd seen before in another lifetime. The three-course lunches, Montségur, Minèrve. Renne-le-Chateau. Le shopping. Rosé O'clock. Feeling home and safe in my body with Mary Magdalene surrounding us. Meeting new, lifelong, sister-friends…and most of all, the beautiful churches *everywhere* dedicated to her.

After Wendy and I met, the ball started rolling. There was a free online writing retreat with Kathleen McGowan and Astara Jane Ashley, publisher of Flower of Life Press. *What? Are you kidding me?* I signed up for their nine-month *Divine Writing Journey*. In the container of this sacred sisterhood, I took a deep dive into writing my healing memoir. Astara Jane Ashley was also on my Sacred France trip. We wept together at ancient Cathar sites, tears pouring out of our cells. Several of the tour participants had also gone through another program, called *Beauty Unleashed*, where they learned to embody shakti and the sacred feminine. Plus, they looked dazzling at breakfast each morning eating their chocolate croissants. I signed up for the course. Anahita Joon, course creatrix, offered a writing contest midway through the program with Flower of Life Press. The winner would gain a spot in the Anthology you now hold in your hands.

I won the contest.

Two months ago, Astara reached out and asked me to join the team at Flower of Life Press. I accepted! Sure, I still work the day jobs, but maybe not forever. Lord knows, there are still tough moments; it's not a life with job security (turns out, old people, bless their hearts, die). But, I'm alive with gratitude for being a writer where even the craziest moments are fodder for my work. I am on my path and excited to share my spiritual memoir with others who've walked in my shoes. I am working toward becoming a career writer. The sacred container of the Divine Feminine now enfolds me every day.

Sister, what I want to tell you is this: *Keep moving forward.*

Even when there's no visible, obvious reason to trust that things will change. Pray fervently with all your heart for that thing aligned most with your Soul. And then offer it up. Let go. Let it come in its own time. Mostly, believe someone's listening.

They are listening.

FREE GIFT

My Gift to You:

I am pleased to offer **the first chapter of my upcoming book, *Girl Remembered: a Memoir of Trauma, Healing, and Grace,*** releasing in 2023.

In this chapter, you will be introduced to my childhood home—a place so warm and idyllic, that the reader must stretch their imagination to grasp a devastating trauma that occurred there. The chapter begins the story of my lifelong journey—with my angels and divine guides—to heal.

To access, visit **girlremembered.com**

CARYL ANNE ENGEL'S *upcoming book,* Girl Remembered: A Memoir of Trauma, Healing, and Grace *will be released in 2023. Caryl's passion is using her voice and life experience, with humor, to help others heal. Caryl's gift is elucidating the Soul's path in shaping our life story. She has been on a lifelong journey to understand this phenomenon. Her joy is sharing this wisdom with her readers.*

Caryl's spiritual counseling practice is Angel Speak. She communicates with Angels and discerns a clients' Soul purpose as it relates to their gifts, talents, and life themes. Numerology, mediumship work, and past life readings guide her sessions. For Caryl, writing books and public speaking on these topics has become her life mission.

When not writing and speaking, Caryl enjoys hiking in nature, photography, creating mosaics in her art studio, gardening, and traveling to sacred sites in Europe. Her happy place is in the kitchen baking pies. Caryl learned early on that cultivating a sense of humor will get you through just about anything.

Caryl is Executive Assistant to the Publisher/CEO at Flower of Life Press. Though she has lived in Northern California for thirty years, she still misses summer thunderstorms off Lake Erie from her childhood.

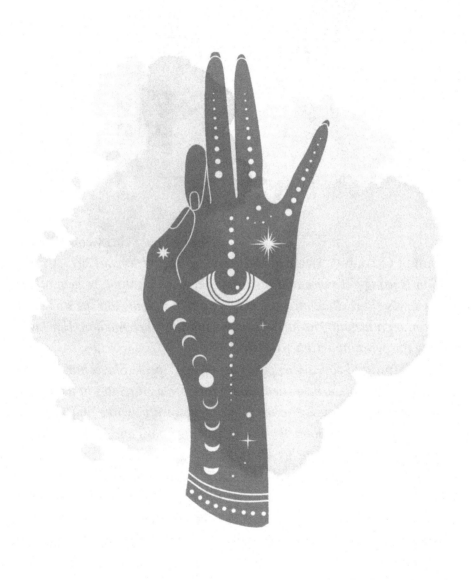

Chapter 9

Following my *InnHer* Voice

By Katie Fink

She has many names—intuition, inner knowing, gut feeling, internal voice.

I like to call her my *InnHer* voice.

Since I can remember, this voice has been deeply clear to me—she speaks to me through my heart, with symbols, synchronicities, numbers, and visions. This wise, higher self always has my truest needs and spiritual desires in mind and I hear her as I navigate about my days. You may have heard this voice in your life, too.

She's been with me since I can remember, always guiding me, and forever focused on my best interests as she leads me to fulfill my destiny. As a kid, I listened to her with ease, like another parent in my life. During my teenage years, I negotiated with her as peer pressure crept in—I'd want to stay at a party until midnight and she would guide me towards an early bedtime so I could be at my best for my 5 am rowing practice. At pivotal moments she spoke to me in signs and saved me from danger several times. When I asked her where I should attend college, she promptly put three very clear cues in my path within an hour.

As the years went on, she became the friend I could always call on. We picked right back up where we left off—she never judged me for my lapses in communication with her and always welcomed me back home into her big, beautiful heart of light. Although I've always heard her voice in the background, I didn't always follow her (even when her nudges were loud and persistent).

This is a story about my journey that led me to follow her with my whole self. But the story must start with the crumbling that occurred when I didn't heed her wisdom.

The house was on a pristine pond in a quaint New England town. The location was perfect on paper, but in reality, the home's glory days were far behind it, physically crumbling and in need of an abundance of renovations.

As I drove up the long driveway to our new house, something felt off inside my body. Leading up to this move, I had felt it over and over. I knew that this new home was not going to cure this sickening feeling inside my body, but I continued to hope that my *InnHer* voice was wrong. "It's going to be great," I reasoned with myself. I wanted to believe my own self-talk, but my body felt the urge to turn the car around and unwind this new home purchase.

This was only the beginning of the crumbling.

Pulling up to the house, I was met by the former owner, charging toward me and screaming with rage, "This is not your house. Get out. Get out. Get out." How I wished I had listened to my voice's message in the months that followed. Leading up to the signing of the purchase and sales statement, my *InnHer* voice gave me countless opportunities to exit the deal, but I kept pushing her aside.

A few weeks before signing for the house, she encouraged me to have an honest conversation with my husband, saying, Before you do this, ask him the question on your mind. So one night, I did.

"Before we buy this home," I said with trepidation, "I need to ask you something. I think something is deeply wrong, and I think you are using drugs. If you are, please tell me now so we can get you help, and let's not buy this house."

He assured me he would never use drugs and his charisma worked its magic to make me believe that all was well. Maybe he was drinking a little too much but he would cut back, he promised, telling me that all was going to be wonderful. But the constant sniffing and peculiar behavior nagged at me.

In time, we moved in. But I was hesitant to unpack many of the boxes as my *InnHer* voice told me not to. I wasn't sure why until months later when the decay set in and our lives began to unravel.

My house and marriage weren't the only stressors in my life. My son experienced a severe and rare bacteria that affected the middle of his right ear, which would go on to require several surgeries at Mass Eye and Ear in Boston—some as long as eight hours in the ER with his surgeon and infectious disease doctor at Mass General. As I recall my first meeting with the infectious disease doctor, I vividly remember him entering the room, saying, "This is not what you want to hear from your child's doctor, but I'm taking on your son's case because it is deeply interesting and unique."

I often wonder if this manifested for my son because he didn't want to hear what was transpiring around him. My daughter started having nightmares the minute we moved in. Even our sweet dog began to physically waste away. And my husband? He was becoming more and more absent every day. He was physically present but emotionally distant. Soon, he spiraled into a deep addiction, and several car accidents in a short time period made it clear that my *InnHer* voice had been correct. My husband was an addict.

The house itself never became a home. It was deteriorating alongside my sweet family.

On the outside, who would know? We seemed like a picture-perfect post-card—beautiful family, great jobs, amazing young kids. But inside, there was a deep pain. For me, it was the pain of isolation. I didn't feel I could share my story with anyone. How could I tell them my concerns about my husband's drug problem? How could I tell them that I suspected there was more to the car accidents than he led me to believe?

It was in this home, in this pain, that my numbness set in. My hands and feet would often go numb, which I later learned was caused by repressing my emotions and not listening to my *InnHer* voice. On top of this numbness, my body was broken with chronic low back pain, hip pain, and the profound exhaustion of trying to save everyone from this wild spiral.

I was becoming stagnant in my physical vessel—my body was screaming for help. At night, I would get the kids to bed and then I would lay in my bed and pretend to be asleep, hoping that my husband would not come in and wake me. The numbness would start and I would resist Googling all the terrible reasons my body felt this way. I would lie there thinking, "There has to be a better way. This cannot be our life."

The days spent holding everything together for my family and working as an executive at a Fortune 100 company were taxing. But the nights were the worst—painful and terrorizing.

One day, when I could no longer take the pain, I left the house and stepped outside. I knelt on the soft ground, and I prayed, and I prayed, and I prayed. I said, "Please, God, Goddess Sophia, the Divine, please show me that there is a path forward." I promised then that I would listen to my *InnHer* voice. I just needed help with the first step.

"Please show me another way!" I pleaded. And with that cry for help, an invitation to a local women's circle came to me the next day. I can't remember the exact words in the email, but they deeply resonated, asking, "Are you broken? Do you need women to gather with?"

I did.

I started attending this local women's circle at the beautiful Temple of Remembrance near my home in Massachusetts and began my journey to wholeness. It was there that I learned to Awaken the Divine® within myself.

The proprietress of the temple was a Priestess and now a beloved friend. We gathered in her beautiful space in the woods where everyone sat on the floor in a circle. I was too broken to sit on the floor. My back, my hips, and the numbness would seize me. With shame, I asked to sit in a chair while the others gathered on the floor, and we would share our stories. We began with one woman's story, which gently weaved into another. With these women, I discovered that I could be raw and vulnerable—I could share in my fullness in this safe circle. In that circle, I received the first pings of remembrance—recollections I had gathered in circles in past lifetimes.

What I love the most about a circle is that nobody responds: they only listen and hold space for you. You can cry, you can share with blissful vulnerability, or you can say nothing at all. As I sat in the circle, I broke down in tears. I cried and cried as I shared my story and my sisters witnessed me. Perhaps my story triggered some women and perhaps it gave others permission to use their voices, too.

As I continued to meet in this circle, I learned to trust my *InnHer* voice again. This tender and wise voice has always had my back. My *InnHer* was right 100% of the time. She tried to tell me so many times not to buy the house. She told me my husband had an addiction. She told me there was a better future. (Later, she would tell me it was time to leave corporate America. But that's another story for another time.)

On this temple floor, I found myself again. I've always been obsessed with understanding the mysteries of the universe but had buried this curiosity over the years because mysticism was seen as taboo. It was weird. Uncomfortable for people in my life. But on this temple floor, I felt seen and heard, and I began to find my own voice again.

As life on the outside continued to unravel at an alarming pace, the temple was a way to escape to another world and regain the strength I needed for the world I faced every day.

Then our anniversary weekend arrived. The kids were with my parents and I was waiting at home for my husband to arrive to have a nice celebration. I spoke to him on the phone and noticed his words were a little slurred. I asked him, "Have you been drinking?"

"No. Of course not," he said.

My *InnHer* voice told me otherwise and I pleaded, "Please just stay where you are and I will come pick you up."

He never made it home that night.

I spent hours driving through the streets between where we lived and where he told me he was, without success. I looked for car accidents and cars down ditches, knowing something was terribly wrong.

Eventually, I phoned a close friend to be with me at the house. This friend will always hold a sacred place in my heart for being with me during one of my darkest moments. I called the police. I told them my husband was missing. The officer asked a little bit about his history. Did he drink? Did he use drugs?

"Yes, I think perhaps he did." There was no more hiding from the truth.

"Okay," they answered, "We'll find him. Don't worry. Just sit tight. Likely one of the local stations will call us with some news."

This kind police officer came over and sat with us. The officer had been correct, and the local station eventually called to tell us they had my husband. We could go bail him out. My friend and I got in the car and arrived at an unwelcoming police station, where we were met with coldness and judgment. We had done nothing wrong, yet I felt the shame of not having listened to my *InnHer* voice. Perhaps I could have done more, I thought. Perhaps I could have saved him from himself.

Eventually, the police released him to us. He sat silently in the back as we drove home, the stench of alcohol filling the car. We arrived home, my friend left, and then it was just my husband and me. On our anniversary night, there wasn't much to say. I told him I would bring him back to the courthouse the next day and then drop him off at rehab. And I did.

Thankfully, he chose the path of sobriety.

Upon his return from rehab, I invited a Shaman into our home to assist in clearing out all the negative energy. We were gearing up for a major renovation and I needed a clean slate. He went about the home and cleansed and cleared each room and all of us. After the clearing, the Shaman pulled me outside and pleaded with me to wait on the renovation, "Just wait 3 or 4 months and see where your family is at." I did not want to listen, assuring myself that there couldn't be more trauma to come. Yet my *InnHer* voice knew he was right.

The plans for the renovation continued and I had a very clear vision for the kitchen—a white, modern space. When I meditated, a vision of myself in this kitchen would come to me; I saw myself hosting celebratory gatherings. In one vision, I saw myself holding up a beautiful book as I celebrated becoming an author with my friends.

The kitchen we were designing never quite lived up to the kitchen in my vision.

One day, not long after the Shaman's visit, I came home to find a letter on my pillow. My husband had decided to leave. As I held the letter with a shaky hand, I wondered what that meant. Was he just leaving our family? Was he leaving his physical body? Another chaotic night ensued as I tried to track him down, calling his sponsor, his family, and his friends. Where was he? Eventually, we found him safe in a hotel.

I met up with him the next day. I remember asking him, "Can you give just 5% to this family, and I can give the other 95%?"

"No."

"Can you give 1%?"

"No."

And I knew he was right. My *InnHer* voice reminded me that I had promised to listen to her on the day I prayed on the land, and I knew it was time to release this relationship.

She told me there was a full and beautiful life ahead, and so I trusted her during the exhausting days spent working a grueling job in corporate America. I trusted her while I discovered life as a single parent. I trusted her as I mourned the shift in our family unit, when I sold the house, and while I trudged through a divorce.

It was an isolating time in my life, particularly at work, as I experienced a lack of understanding in my workplace while navigating these major life changes. For many, it was easier to just act like business as usual and continue to push and ask for more from me. Leaning into the wisdom of my *InnHer* voice was key for me to know I was worthy of compassion.

Along this journey of change, I began to look for a new home and was drawn to a modern house in a nearby town. I decided to attend an open house, and as I walked through the doors, I saw my kitchen. The kitchen from my vision! I knew then that this would be our healing home.

As I rebuilt my life and the lives of my kids, I also went deep into my inner work to unpack how I lost myself to my relationship, stopped trusting my *InnHer* voice, and lost my own voice somewhere along the way. As I did this *InnHer* work, one constant remained as part of my healing journey— my time at the temple.

Month after month, year after year, I returned to the temple, always finding solace within its sacred walls. I did not lay down and surrender. I rose higher. Until one day, I realized I was whole again.

My back and hip pain and numbness had become a distant memory and I joined my sisters on the temple floor. My capacity for compassion for others was blown wide open as these women continued to share their stories. All too often, we don't know what goes on behind closed doors. I should know. My doors had been closed so tightly.

As I continued to follow my *InnHer* voice, I began to emanate a light that others were seeking. Friends and colleagues would come to me when they were struggling, seeking purpose, or wanting more out of life. My own life changes were sparking something for others to follow.

In February of 2020 while I was seated on the temple floor, I had a significant upload. The message I received was clear: I needed to gather the healers, light workers, mystics, and priestesses together and build a container where they could connect and help more people.

I heard the message deep in my core: Your purpose is to weave this community together so that others may Awaken the Divine® within themselves as you have done. You will create many pathways with the community you gather and show a new path forward, one of wholeness, joy, abundance— this is your birthright.

My immediate thought was, how would I ever do that? I was a single mom with a high-stress job at a Fortune 100 company. How was I going to find time to do that? Who was I to build a mystical lifestyle company? Just one month later, in March of 2020, the world shifted. Out of that chaos emerged just enough extra time and space in my life to make my own shift.

I knew well enough at this point that if I did not listen to my *InnHer* voice, she would keep knocking as she did before. So I listened. I built a magical online marketplace, and synchronicity after synchronicity ensued as I co-created with the universe.

We birthed Mind Body Soul Market in April 2022 and I am overjoyed to see the astounding community that is forming. We have products, classes, and services that support the collective on their wellness and spiritual journeys, and we're able to gather all the mystics, healers, priestesses, psychics, and explorers! Building this business has helped me rediscover my external voice with a newfound vulnerability. Today, I share my story so that it might help other souls find their *InnHer* voice and Awaken the Divine® within themselves.

After launching mindbodysoulmarket.com, I found myself at another crossroads in my corporate life. I was finding it increasingly difficult to stand in my integrity over acceptance, and my *InnHer* voice kept pinging me with her message: choose the path of integrity. For me, the path of integrity meant listening to my *InnHer* voice, standing in my truth and in what I knew was right for me and for my body. As this journey unfolded, I ended up parting ways with my life in corporate America. I chose integrity over acceptance. And my journey continues.

In these past few years, I have learned so much about myself. I've discovered that we can do hard things, and the braver we are, the luckier we are. I know deeply that listening to your *InnHer* voice will always lead you to your soul's mission.

If this resonates with your *InnHer* voice, join us for our Awaken the Divine® series on mindbodysoulmarket.com and explore with our collaborators so you, too, may weave all of your parts together. I became who I am for me, for my soul's satisfaction, and for you.

Today my voice is asking me to make some major quantum leaps. This summer, my *InnHer* voice called me strongly to Avalon to gather with 27 priestesses. There she delivered message after message of what was next, including writing this chapter about my turning point. Her instructions were twofold: (1) raise my vibration, and all else will flow, and (2) play bigger, my love, the collective needs more from you. So bigger I will play—and I hope you'll join me for the ride!

My heart is already filled with gratitude and love as I prepare to stand in my long-awaited modern, white kitchen on December 1st, 2022, to celebrate this book launch.

KATIE FINK *is the Founder and CEO of the recently launched*
MindBodySoulMarket.com *an online marketplace with products, classes and services from exceptional vendors to empower the collective on their wellness and spiritual journeys.*

As a retail tech expert with two decades of experience at a Fortune 100 retailer she has learned career success and a picture perfect life doesn't always translate into a thriving soul. Katie has found her way back to wholeness with the support of wonderful teachers and now her purpose is to support others to awaken the divine within themselves, turn their mess into their magic and glow in their full luminosity!

FREE GIFT

Katie invites you to a free 6-months in her **Luminosity for Light Leaders** subscription on Instagram.

DM **@mindbodysoulmarket** 'luminosity' for details.

With gratitude and love!

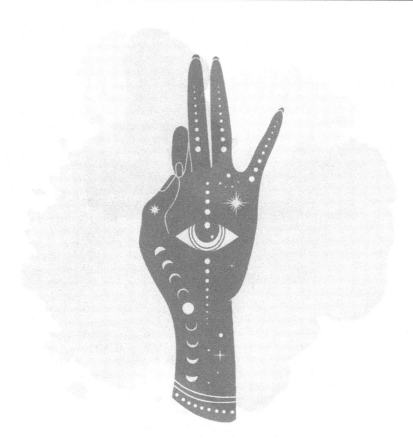

CHAPTER 10

Be Your Own Oracle

By Kristin Ford

Quiet Chaos

I've always hated the sound of my own voice. Some who know me may find that hard to believe, as I am rarely at a loss for words. Yet in many ways, I've spent my life hiding my voice, unnerved by something primordial in its quality and tone. I could hear an echo in it, a calling back to a place my Soul knew, a place that at once fascinated and terrified me. I longed for an effervescent, delicate voice; one that sparkled with innocence and purity. Yet there was little delicacy in my husky, borderline baritone—a man's voice in a little girl's body. A voice that made me different. And different was the one thing I never wanted.

I am the youngest of five children, born two years after my twin sister and brother, six months into the onset of his life-threatening asthma. Mine was a gestation in chaos, as my parents were contending with their son turning blue and needing emergency medical care more often than not. At 42, with five kids under the age of seven, my mom, Roberta, had her hands full. When told that my brother was not expected to live past three years old, she declared, "not on my watch." In measure equal to the uncertainty of his condition, she doubled down on creating order. Rigid, clear-cut rules designed to ensure his survival. Those efforts paid off, keeping him alive until better treatments were available and his own body grew strong enough to manage and eventually outgrow his illness. For me, however, that rigidity was a gilded cage, a perfectly ordered house with no room to breathe. I was a precocious child; my nana described me as, "the other four rolled into one." I didn't get a lot of attention, and with my ebullient nature, the attention I did garner usually wasn't positive. I quickly learned that I was very different from my siblings. Never one to just quietly obey and keep the peace, I questioned everything, and had, in hindsight, a rather ridiculous amount of energy. I was, in a word, non-compliant. I also had an imaginative world that was rich with context and story. I routinely talked to animals, to my dead grandmother, and often left my body energetically to travel in the unseen realms. I was a mystic in the house of reason. I longed to be held and heard, yet when I recounted my experiences, I was chided for lying or exaggerating. I was living a dichotomy of needing to be witnessed while realizing that to be accepted meant not revealing who I am. So, I slipped on my cloak of acceptability and learned to navigate the cage. I chose acceptance over authenticity and unwittingly began a lifelong quest for reunion inside of myself, from a division of my own creation.

Being funny brought somewhat positive attention, and my mother often pointed out it was my saving grace, at least in her eyes. It felt safer to me to make people laugh than be yelled at, so I channeled my abundant energy into being amusing. I was often admonished for performing, yet I was so longing for connection that it was worth the risk. I am an excellent mimic, and it felt far safer to adopt different accents than to say what was real for me. The truth was dangerous, and while I could see it clearly, whenever I spoke my truth, I was either dismissed or silenced. It was easier to slip into a persona than feel the pain of being ignored or attacked. In my young mind, it was clear that made-up voices were welcomed, and that my own strange voice was the problem.

The Path of Deep Resistance

It took me decades to realize the real problem—we don't know what is real without a witness. Growing up in a home where being focused and practical were absolute necessities—Brian's life depended on it—there was little room for my mystical, interior world. I created a division within myself that I alone could not resolve. It wasn't until decades later that I even knew it existed. By that time, I was knee-deep in my practical life, a life that was hell-bent on killing me.

I built my adult life in two silos, one visible to the outside world—practical and successful; the other private, full of mystery and magic. It was a tenuous balance that often skewed way out of alignment. I was in a strange sort of war with myself, and both sides were losing. Yet my soul was persistent. It seemed that for every step I took on the practical path, a Divine grace was offering an equal measure toward my spiritual awakening. This path of duality took root during my college years. I was majoring in accounting—a pragmatic career path by any standard—when late in my freshman year my father died unexpectedly. My world collapsed, and my faith in the illusion of certainty shattered. It was as if everything I had been led to believe about life—about how if you work hard and get a job, get married and have kids, raise them and then retire, then you get to live again and enjoy the fruits of all that labor— that entire construct of what life should be evaporated as my mom, siblings, and I sat by his hospital bed, and she gave permission to turn off my dad's life support. I remember the stillness of his death—the half-gasp and then the quiet, hospital sounds fading as everything in my life coalesced into that one irrevocable moment. Nothing was the same, and yet in the tradition of our family, we were expected to simply carry on as if nothing had changed.

Deeply stunned and not even beginning to understand the process of grieving, I returned to school, studying and working, living in a fog of separation. It was my first experience of how unskilled most of us are at being present to emotion. No one wanted to talk about death or grief, so I went silent and carried on. Thirteen months later, I experienced my first episode of adrenal fatigue. This was also the first of many divine interventions along my journey. In 1986, diagnosed with chronic fatigue, armed with pain medications and antidepressants, I pushed myself to the verge of collapse, until I finally took a semester off from college. Something in me knew there was a different way, so I began my spiritual journey in a most reasonable place, the Occult section of Barnes & Noble. It was there I found hints that my mystical nature was not crazy and that there were so many more options available than the patronizing medical patriarchy. When I returned to college to complete my junior year, I knew I didn't want to be an accountant but resigned myself to finishing my degree. I picked up an English minor because it spoke to my heart, and I set up my life with those same routines and constructs that I had learned as a child. My health was precarious, and I limited my life to only the tasks that were necessary. I was now in a different cage, isolated in a body that constantly betrayed me, drifting further from my voice as I ventured out into the world.

For a couple of years, I floundered, the recurring fatigue limiting my life and work options. A bad economy and lack of motivation found me bouncing from temp job to temp job, not using my education and feeling less and less like I had anything to offer. On the surface it seemed as if I was coping, going out more with friends and trying to have a normal life, immersing myself in the arcane and alternative in my free time, watching my nephew at night while my sister worked, and trying to not nap half the day. The true light in my life was my friend Chris, whom I had known since childhood. Our families vacationed together for years, and from the time we were young, it was clear that there was something magical about our connection. He was my soulmate, a term I had recently learned and barely understood. We had a silent knowing of each other, a bond that was evolving as we were, always orbiting back in the direction of each other. Chris emanated light and was the one person who never shrank from my inner darkness. He stood by me in it, offering me a depth of wisdom and compassion that revealed his timeless soul. I wanted to spend my life with him. When he died at 22, I was hollowed. The soundless wail of my soul reverberated from the core of my being to the heart of the cosmos.

There is something about disbelief that allows us to continue when everything we rely on shatters. The mundane activities, the routines of normalcy, and the bars of my cage became my salvation. At 24 years old, for the second time in my life, I was shattered by grief and carried by the Divine. A week after his death, I was offered a temporary job working on a medical device recall. Numb and reeling, I said yes. Grace comes in many forms, and this divine intervention led to the beginning of my accounting career and meeting one of my dearest friends. Yet the path was not clear, and I had much to learn about the perils of my two lives.

When I was deciding on what to major in at college, my mother encouraged accounting, as it was a "good career for women." I'm still not sure what that means, but it was the 80s, and honestly, it was something that came easily to me. I'd taken a bookkeeping course in high school, and it just made sense. Accounting is actually quite Zen—an elegant system in which everything must balance and be equal. That it was the foundation of my professional life for over 20 years is not surprising, given that my early upbringing was centered around maintaining a semblance of balance amidst the chaos. In the aftermath of Chris' death, I found strange salvation in my work. It turned out that there was something in my life that I could control: making sure the debits and credits balanced and that the financial statements went out on time. These were odd blessings that kept my inner chaos monkey at bay. I excelled at work and privately swung between heavily self-medicating with food and alcohol and learning everything I could about reiki, meditation, healing—anything that offered some solace. The two silos were in full battle mode, and the motto of my life at the time was "soldier on." I was thirsty for answers, for knowledge, for anything that would water the silenced mystic, that would grant me a brief semblance of feeling normal. I collected certificates in various modalities and eventually found myself guided to earn a Master's in Spiritual Psychology.

My workaholic self was in full swing, my personal life a hot mess, but my dedication to self-discovery, to observing and actively participating in my own evolution of consciousness, was finally gaining ground. I could sense a different pathway, a possibility of something I could not yet name. I could once again hear the old echo, that unnerving quality that had frightened me as a child. This time it would not be silenced. By the time I had my second adrenal collapse in 2016, I knew I needed to bridge these two worlds or I would not survive. My body was railing against the endless hours of uninspired, often thankless work, my knees were breaking down, and I was exhausted; always the life of the party on the outside, and in deep anguish on the inside. I was dying by degrees. I had done so much internal work, therapy, self-discovery, working my process, and I knew there was more to life than how I was living. I was closer, yet not quite living in integrity with my Self. I just couldn't find a way off the damn hamster wheel.

Deconstructing the Cage

My breaking point was in 2019. Three years after I quit my corporate finance career, started a construction company with a friend, built a lucrative private accounting practice, had three surgeries in a year and a near-fatal post-op infection, I was coming undone. And then my 94-year-old mother had a stroke that left her with no short-term memory and sliding into dementia. While my sister, Beth, had for years been devoted to my mom's physical care, I knew I was the only one in our family equipped to accompany her on the spiritual journey of her transition. In fact, I knew that was why I was her daughter. It was our soul agreement. I recognized that this was also her final gift to me—my exit strategy from a life I no longer recognized. As I deconstructed my work life in order to be with her, I entered a new kind of separate world. I was witnessing my mom, yet she was more and more detached from my physical world reality. Our time was spent in an energetic dance, as she wove between this world and beyond. I anchored myself in my presence with her, spending evenings and weekends in her cozy, book-filled den. She sheltered in her favorite chair, reveling in having her dinner brought in for her and asking why I was always around, while I stationed myself on the loveseat, present to her shifting reality, and ever vigilant for that inevitable moment of her last breath.

Home improvement shows and NCIS episodes were the backdrop to our conversations, which slipped from somewhat lucid reminiscence into the hazy world of dementia. As a person who has lived her life in between energetic worlds, this was at once familiar and completely unknown territory. The months passed in this sacred vigil, and I was further disconnected from the life I had built for myself. As with my earlier experiences with death and grief, only a few dear friends understood, and my social circle dissipated. In my deepening isolation, I longed for conversation and witnessing. It seemed like the world outside our bubble was filled with idle chatter, strife, and discord. I felt unable to speak out, silently suffocating in my strange new world. My mom transitioned in November 2019, and I felt both at peace and deeply exhausted. I craved depth and intimacy, yet felt little connection to what used to feel familiar. I hesitantly ventured out into what was left of my former life, and slowly began to pick up the pieces. The

Pandemic, however, had other ideas. Into shutdown I went, with the dual goals of resting my body, and of reconnecting my soul.

Living alone during Covid, I was determined to create more support for myself. I hosted far too many zoom meetings, participated in a women's prosperity circle, and deepened core friendships with my Covid Coven. I was finding my voice again, and in the safety of these circles, began to realize that those around me were truly hearing my heart. And they looked to me to lead the conversation. It was also clear that they shared my frustration with the constant discord that seemed to rule the daily narratives. I knew that what we needed was a different conversation, and yet I felt totally unsafe speaking outside my own circle. It seemed like only the loudest voices were heard, and those who sought answers wanted a quick fix, a leader or guru who claimed to solve our problems for us. I knew the answers I sought were inside me, and yet I was still hesitant to use my own voice to speak them.

I believe that we are all part of a cosmic intelligence, an intelligence accessible within each one of us. I also see that we are distracted from this inner knowing by the competing narratives that bombard us every day, convincing us to remain in our silos. I know that if we trust ourselves enough to honor and accept who we are, in our unique radiance, that we will be able to honor and accept others for their light. In the strange circumstance of the pandemic, I finally found the answer to the division I had created within myself. My voice was never the problem. I had a visibility issue. I lived in so much isolation that I lacked true witnessing—I could not see myself for the Radiantly Divine Human Being I am. And I realized that to be truly witnessed by someone else, I needed the courage to be fully seen and heard. I needed to be my own Oracle.

The challenge is that collectively we've forgotten how to filter out all the noise and trust the power of our own unique song. We hold misperceptions that the right teachings or trappings are needed to explore our inner world; that purchasing the right spiritual commodity will solve everything. What I found is another path, a more direct way to facilitate integration within. I witness. I hold space and guide, channeling the cosmos in support of the full expression of our Divine Humanity. I recognize the interconnectedness of all beings, as I now recognize my mother's voice in my own. What frightened me as a child about my own voice, that ancient and primordial quality, I now understand as the power of my Sacred Masculine, ever vigilant, holding sanctuary within me for the re-emergence of my ancestral Divine Feminine. It is a legacy of generations of women silenced, beseeching me to be their voice. In healing the divide within myself, they now speak through me in Union, a harmonious voice, resonant and sovereign. Invoking their strength as I claim my own, I choose my Voice, the voice of the Oracle.

FREE GIFT

My Gift to You:

A guided meditation focused on embodiment and inspired by the sovereignty of the hawk.

To access, visit **www.infinitewisdomcollective.com**

KRISTIN FORD *has always been a mystic, experiencing realms and energies that are unseen, weaving worlds into being in her consciousness. Although she hid these intuitive gifts while building a successful and remarkably practical career in finance and consulting, her life experiences made it clear that she needed to honor her intuition as deeply as her intellect. Her lifelong journey to give her inner mystic a voice led Kristin to explore various healing modalities, earn a Master's in Spiritual Psychology, and to found Infinite Wisdom Collective. As a spiritual mentor, Kristin uses her voice and a process of deep witnessing to guide clients to their unique self-expression.*

Kristin currently lives on Boston's North Shore, where she draws inspiration from the woods and the wild Atlantic. A self-described "accidental photographer," Kristin also spends her free time traveling, writing, developing her new podcast, Wisdom & Wonder, and trying to not set off the smoke alarm every time she cooks.

Follow Kristin on these platforms:

www.infinitewisdomcollective.com
www.facebook.com/InfiniteWisdomCollective
www.instagram.com/infinitewisdomcollective
www.patreon.com/kristinmford
www.infinitewisdomcollective.com/about-the-author

CHAPTER 11

Trauma as a Portal to Soul Alignment

By Kirsty Jandrell

"Kirsty, both our parents are dead."

It was 1:40 a.m. on a Tuesday morning when I received the phone call from my stepsister.

My world stopped. I remember the absurdity of the scenario, and I believe that a fragment of my soul left my body at that precise moment. I struggled, as anybody would, to comprehend what I was hearing. Just before falling asleep, I had been writing in my gratitude diary, blissfully unaware of what had occurred earlier that evening.

Many times, I recount the circumstances of their deaths. The horrifically surreal nature of the event never fails to take my breath away. My stepfather suffered a huge cardiac arrest while preparing dinner. My mom managed to alert the emergency services. When the paramedics arrived, she was lying on the hall floor. She managed to crawl to the front door to let them in. They promptly called a second ambulance vehicle, as it appeared that she was also in cardiac arrest after falling down the stairs, (while on the phone with the emergency services, we believe). Those brave health worker angels attempted to revive them both simultaneously. My stepfather was pronounced dead while still home, and my mom was declared passed upon arriving to the hospital. They transitioned within thirty minutes of each other. Both were considered in "good health" prior to this event.

Due to a quirk of geography, they were taken to two separate chapels of rest about ten miles apart. I visited both on the day after they passed, in between making what must have amounted to dozens of phone calls to friends and family to inform them of what had happened. With each call, I tried to soften the double blow somehow for the recipient, empathizing with the shock of what they were hearing.

It was the day after Mother's Day in the UK. For the first time in 46 years, I did not spend it with my mom. Despite my many pleas for her to join us for Sunday lunch, she insisted that it was now "Your time to be a mom on Mother's Day." She had often referred to my husband as my "knight in shining armour." She was full of fun and sass, and she had the biggest heart. The week prior, my daughter and I spent what was to be our last day with her. We met for lunch, just the three of us, as a premature Mother's Day meal. I still look at photographs we took that day, her smile huge, her eyes twinkling, and her 74-year-old skin glowing. I visited her in the hospital chapel of rest for a second time the day after they passed, hoping this would help me to process the impossible. Her hands, which she had always taken great care of, were still beautiful. I could not kiss her "goodbye," it was too much to bear.

Usually, I sent my mom a "goodnight" text, with her usual loving sign off being "Ni' Night, see you in the morning!" Throughout my life, she was my rock, my touchstone, indeed pretty much a marker for all I did. She was always there for me to comfort and steady me through life's ups and downs. She was at my side each step of my fertility journey, which my husband and I were on in the six years prior to our only child's birth. Ultimately, she was delighted to become a grandmother at the ripe age of 72. My stepfather was also a soulmate, and I grew ever so close to him over the quarter of a century that they were together. Now, they were gone, in tandem, in one instant. No more.

I am writing this as I lie on one of my favourite Welsh beaches, the Cambrian hills as my backdrop, echoing the Goddesses' curves as she reclines facing the ocean, her form providing the structure for waves of emotion echoing the fluidity of this scene. The liminal space.

I heard the siren call from the divine feminine in December of 2018, five months before my parents' deaths. Although I have experienced a rich spiritual life since childhood, I always side-lined this passion and this often-times intensely private "me" in favour of the life I felt I was duty-bound to lead: as a student, athlete, postgraduate, once times party girl, and latterly successful entrepreneur and businesswoman. I was a late bloomer in terms of "settling down," married to my beloved finally at the age of 44 and elated to be a first-time mum at 46. I was always somewhat of a free spirit at heart, always questioning societal norms, especially where inequality, bigotry, and unfairness raised their ugly heads.

My flower fairy spirit was never far from the surface, despite having spent the majority of my adult life working in corporate environments, Bauhaus-style office blocks, and the epitome of capitalist individualism of the 1980s: the structurally impressive, but soulless, Canary Wharf development in London.

Born into a hardworking and "respectable" working class family in the industrial Midlands of England during the 1970s, I was nurtured so lovingly by my family and never wanted for anything, love and emotional support being ever present. However, the backdrop of economic depression prior to Thatcher's Britain was pervasive. The cultural "fear" of falling out of favor of the system and the scarcity narrative in which I grew up, served as a constant reminder that you became as well-educated as possible and secured a career that would provide financial stability and societal approval. And so it was for me. Training as a primary school teacher, then establishing a recruitment company, I was "successful" in that narrow sense of the word, making my parents proud, and giving me a sense of material security.

In December of 2018, however, my inner voice, calling me to spiritual freedom and to make a real difference in the world, was getting louder. Over the last few years, I had continued to pursue further spiritual trainings, qualifying as a life coach, and completed several healing courses, which has allowed me to quench this desire and add to my ever-expanding "spiritual toolbox." My "side-line" passion is yoga, which I have practiced and taught for over twenty years. But at that point, I decided I just had to finally figure out what I had incarnated to do! What was my soul purpose, and just as importantly, how was I going to embody this while still being able to dedicate myself to my most important roles as mum and wife, business owner, and employer? This wasn't going to be clear-cut!

What shifted at this point, however, was the gnosis and indeed, the urgency I felt in this awareness. I had an understanding that our planet, our beloved Mamma Gaia, was in deep crisis, and that we were in a profound period of transition. However, I managed to quiet the call yet again, not with as much conviction as previously, but in the sense that I would just allow this to work through me in divine timing and simply allow it all to unfold.

Then, on April 1st, 2019, my world turned upside down. To start with, I coped as best I could, which was by existing in a state of complete denial of the magnitude of the event. I stuffed down the pain with poor nutritional choices and general busyness. I continued on my path as a spiritual seeker with more intensity than before, but in doing so, failed to deal with the grief, in the mistaken belief that I had to "hold it together" for my beloved daughter, who was eighteen months old at the time, for my husband, and for my employees.

I could not afford to "fall apart." Who would take care of our daughter and my business? With my parents gone and us as 'geriatric parents,' our childcare options had virtually disappeared with them.

I couched my loss in words of gratitude. Gratitude has been such a powerful practice for so long and has served me so well. It has allowed me to sink into the unconditional love and support of the benevolent, ever-expanding, and abundant universe. In this case, however, it saw me spiritually bypassing the trauma I had experienced and provided me with an excuse not to face it. Using spirituality as a shield, while allowing my wound to fester.

My mantras became…"I'm just so grateful they didn't suffer/they went together as they were soulmates/they got to meet and spend time with their granddaughter." I genuinely felt thankful for the fact that they transitioned quickly and together, but focusing on that prevented me from facing the depth of grief that lay beneath. I was disconnected. The only true joy I allowed myself to experience was through my beloved daughter. It was only in her presence that I let my guard down and even occasionally allowed myself to cry, but even then, only with restraint. There was no weeping, no rage, no screaming…just mild sadness being expressed. I was able to convey some of my heartbreak to my endlessly supportive husband but I was afraid he might struggle with the depth of my raw grieving, so I self-monitored these outpourings, too. In the early days after their deaths, I visited a grief counselor, but after a few months, I declared that I was "fine" and didn't require any further care. Nothing could have been further from the truth.

This went on for several years. On the surface, all seemed well—my parents' house was sold, our daughter was happy and thriving, and my business and my husband's survived, despite all the pandemic could throw at them. We were both so grateful, as many had been less fortunate.

Slowly, however, my spark began to fade. I felt as if I was emerging from the grieving process, yet I was walking through life completely out of touch with my feelings…uncomfortably numb and paralyzed in fear of peeling back any emotional scars, in case Pandora's box of angry blackbirds would be unleashed and I might drown in a lake of my own tears as a consequence.

The essence of it was that my wild, free, and enthusiastic inner child my mom had so deeply loved and encouraged in all things, had left. The façade that remained was a sensible, sanitized, and polite version of me, who was walking through her duties day to day, scared shitless that she might lose the remaining precious elements in her life. On the outside, I was "coping" beautifully. Concerned, loving friends and family asked my abundantly patient husband how I was doing. "She's okay; she's coping well," were his stock responses. No one would dare ask me directly how I was feeling.

The process of finally acknowledging that this trauma and grief was screaming out to be processed and healed was gradual. As menopause layered its own peculiar brand of challenges into the cauldron of complex emotional soup, I felt as though I was slowly drowning in the quicksand of unresolved anger, fear, and pain, which simply refused to go away.

Then I took the step of receiving therapy from some amazing healers, and slowly, the tight ball of energetic stuckness started to unravel, with fragments of my wholeness slowly beginning to surface to be healed and transformed—in a safe container. Gradually the magic started to unfold.

Slowly, ever so slowly, my joy and passion began to return. And with it came a new awareness. I had realised that all I required to heal lay inside me; I just needed to access it. No more did I constantly look for my value in others' eyes. Gradually I began to start to reconnect. Not whole *again*, but whole for the first time in my life!

I now look inside for answers. I look to my heart, and if in doubt, ask my spiritual guides—my "divine team." Knowing in a very real and somatic sense that all the answers lie within is life changing. My heart, like many, has been broken many times, but each time it is knitted back together by love, it becomes simultaneously more resilient and more compassionate.

And this is the true revelation of my turning point story: that the process of self-healing though trauma is the portal through which opportunities and light can flow and expand. As I connected to my "self," my inner truth, my North Star, and acknowledged—even welcomed—the shadow elements of the soul to the party, the easier it became to integrate into wholeness. No more running away. No more numbing out. No more pretending that everything is always 'okay'. Being comfortable in admitting that sometimes, it isn't.

As this started to unfold, my intuitive gifts as a healer, a channel, a priestess, and a lightworker started to blossom. I truly began to re-member who I was and what I had been sent here to do. I was offered opportunities to hold ceremonial spaces and to engage in healing and further study as my path became more clear.

The real watershed moment, the nexus point, occurred In Avalon (Glastonbury, UK), at the beginning of the Lion's Gate portal in July 2022, the day before my mom's birthday. I found myself in the presence of one of my beloved mentors, whose power and unconditional love for me as a transmission of the divine feminine, shook me to the core. This was my first time experiencing an "in-person" temple space, and I was not fully pre-pared for the profundity of the event, and all that was to follow. In a circle of sisters, I stood forward and allowed my truths to be uttered. Speaking from my heart, I cried, laughed, and shook from the palpable energy of the process. I was held by the love of the other souls in the room—both seen and unseen—as they witnessed me. I was in true community, bathing in love from the Goddess, the Great Mother who holds us all.

That day I stepped forward and stepped up to meet myself. Working in partnership, I declared to my higher self that *"By Samhain (31st October), I plan to step away from the day-to-day running of my business and take steps to allow for my sacred work to develop."* By mid-August, and perhaps not coincidentally on the closing day of the Lion's gate portal, this happened. My successor couldn't have been more thrilled to take on a new role and new responsibilities within my company. For me, the feelings of liberation and possibility are incredible. Plus, this was all done with grace, love, and true gratitude, and with the intent of being for the highest good for all.

As of writing this, I have transitioned and stepped into my sacred work by holding my first ceremonial women's circle, holding one to one healing sessions, and am ready for so much more to develop. I am poised to allow inspiration, guidance, and clarity to flow through me and so that I may continue to step in and open up to the path of service I was destined to pursue. I am filled with light, energy, joy, hope, and anticipation, as opposed to feeling held down, overwhelmed, stressed, anxious, and depressed.

Finally, I have been able to stand in integrity as a healer and hold space for others as they seek to align with their true purpose and find a connection with their authentic selves. I now stand in integrity and say, *"I have walked through the fire, and I have emerged stronger and more compassionate, and now I am able to hold you unconditionally, in love and healing."*

There is also a peace that has evolved around my parents' death. I know they are always supporting me and my loved ones—their family. In fact, mom sent the following message through one of my mentors, a few weeks after her death:

"I am in the birds, I am in the song, I am in the breeze."

I carry this with me everywhere and feel her loving presence beside me, always. My parents often make themselves known to me, as a pair of buzzards flying high above our house in the Welsh hillside. Their sightings always bring a smile and a giggle to me, my husband, and my daughter.

If you are in unresolved grief from the loss of a loved one, I wish to reassure you that they are always with you, and you can always access their support—you just have to ask. Often the assistance I have been given from the other side has been more powerful and impactful than anything my parents could have offered while they were on the physical plane. Whenever

I am about to move into a potentially challenging situation, I ask for their assistance, and always feel held.

I truly believe that from the brokenness of trauma and grief, it is possible to view a portal which invites you to deepen into your intuition, self-reliance, and sovereignty. This entryway also provides an opportunity to shed the masks that have not been serving you, as you step into your integrity and align with your essence.

It also allows you to release that which no longer serves you, to "de-clutter" your life and re-prioritize the crucial elements, and spend your time with people and in activities that light you up rather than drain you. As you shift and uplevel, your vibration elevates, and relationships and circumstances that once held you back will just fall away with love and grace.

As you open to the ocean of divine love, compassion, and joy, opportunities for evolution and beauty will flow into your energetic field—once you start to allow them to.

I do not pretend that this is an easy process, or a linear one. But patience, trust, self-compassion and focus render it a beautiful spiral dance to weave.

The world needs YOU to vibrate in alignment with your essential resonance. As we transition to the new earth, however this unfolds, your light is needed to illuminate the way. As you start to heal, your beautiful soul will be bathed in the purest light, and then you can radiate your love and compassion out like a beacon of the loving energy you are!

So, if you are still grappling with unresolved trauma or grief, friend, I want to lovingly reassure you that by taking the next step on your healing journey, you are not only moving towards your soul's liberation but towards more joy, purpose, abundance, and peace than might ever seem possible.

Grief does not have to be the end, it can also be a gateway, a marker on your soul's evolutionary journey.

I wish you only love as I walk beside you, as indeed, we all walk each other home.

"May the long-time sun shine above you, may all love surround you.
May the pure light within you, guide your way on."
—Mike Heron, from 'Long Time Sun'

KIRSTY JANDRELL *is an entrepreneur, business owner, ceremonial priestess, yoga teacher, transformational coach and healer. As a former teacher and founder of an ethical recruitment company, she is now blessed to be living in soul alignment, by guiding women to realize a life of authenticity, joy and soul purpose! Two initiations, (becoming a first-time mom at 46, then losing both her parents in their sudden transition a year later), served as a wakeup call, leading her to follow her heart, her passion and her North Star, and help others to do the same.*

An original free spirit and flower fairy child, she can be found living and playing with her beloved husband and daughter in the rural hills of Wales, alongside their fur babies, Shanti and Iggy, the Shelties and George, the tolerant tabby cat! You can contact her at **www.kirstyjandrell.com** *or through her Facebook Group, The Creatrix Collective.*

FREE GIFT

My Gift to You:

5 Minutes to Ground, Calm, and Protect Your Energy!

With this beautiful PDF you will receive an audio activation and bodywork and breathing practices, which will prepare you to embrace your day with positivity, clarity, and alignment—in just 5 minutes!

To access, visit **kirstyjandrell.pages.ontraport.net/5-min-free-gift**

CHAPTER 12

From Feral Child to Wild Woman

By Christina Mercy, LCSW CHt RYT200

Imagine you are holding an antique telescope, feeling the polished gold and brass in your hands. You notice it has a large aperture to see a great distance. Your hands outline the intricate carvings etched into the leather binding. It's a mysterious apparatus and has the unusual ability of granting the viewer a look back in time. With curiosity, you take a peek. Focusing your eye, a bright light begins to appear. As your eyes adjust, you can see a young woman lying on the floor. How did she end up in this unconscious state? Her body has lost all consciousness; a friend is kneeling beside her. Noticing the paraphernalia, you can somehow intuit she overdosed on cocaine, and quickly sum up she must be dead. Her friend is shaking her, speaking her name. She does not respond; she does not wake up. Suddenly, the brilliant bright light returns while the images fade into the past.

Incidentally, 911 was called and the friend ran. Miraculously she awoke. It wasn't her time to go just yet; she had a lot of living to do. Her heart was broken from her recent divorce; they had been in relationship since she was 13. She also had three children to raise. Not realizing it at the time, she was actually experiencing a powerful awakening. As she grasped her breath, a knowing materialized. Her body could not take this route of escape any longer. Her nickname was Tina. This seemed to have happened a lifetime ago—metaphorically, a past life. It took a few more months for her to trust there was a better way to live.

Embodying the Womb Wound

Allow me to back up and share a piece of science called epigenetics. When my grandmother was pregnant with my mother, I was an egg in my mother's womb. The research has concluded that DNA from our grandmothers, mothers, and matriarchal lineage carries codes and messages and can carry traumatic cellular memory. What has surprised and interested me about my cellular imprints and DNA history is the knowledge of my grandmother, mother, and most of my family's experience of sexual abuse. My life growing up was a hot mess. As a spirit being, I began forming as an egg inside my mother's womb, at a precise exact moment in time when one of my father's sperms made its way to spark a cataclysmic formation. What was one cell suddenly merged into two, and formed a symbol referred to as a Vesica Pisces—it's all part of the mysterious sacred geometry linked with creative science. Very quickly, the two cells divided further, creating what resembles a Flower of Life. In a few weeks my heart formed, housing my soul, and my physical body began to grow. My spirit chose the physical, because that's what we do as humans: we are actually spiritual beings embodying a physical experience. I have wondered if I knew I was incarnating into a family that had so many struggles. I was created and formed in the womb of a 16-year-old mother and a family who lived at 5 Foster Court in Oakland, California, with a six-foot fence to hide all the secrets. No one could peek through the windows and see what was really happening inside.

Her/story vs. His/tory

Adverse childhood experiences led me to a drug overdose at age 29. Years later, I discovered I was experiencing what astrologers refer to as a Saturn Return. This cycle happens every 28-30 years and can last for three years. Saturn was teaching my soul and psyche that there was another way to live. Life is filled with possibilities and choices. Saturn is also known as the task master; the teacher bringing lessons and instructing the student to mature and transform through turbulent times. I was at the end of a cycle; this cycle can be referred to as a cosmic turning point. It jolted me out of amnesia.

I kept having a dream with my inner child; she was about two and a half or three years old. She met me wearing a white dress with frilly lace underwear. She was busy coloring while looking out a window. My adult-self talked to her; she did not trust me. I continued to have this dream. Eventually, my inner child self said, "my grandfather touched me." I knew this was true from my family who shared their disturbing, repulsive stories of sexual abuse. Dissociation is a true phenomenon. I had vague memories of instinctively leaving my body for self-preservation. In the past, my grandfather would always deny it when confronted. He would say, "I never touched you kids," or "that's water under the bridge," or, "your mother's crazy." My inner child would not let this go. She wanted answers—she wanted to know the truth! Together we confronted our grandfather during a phone call. We got the full detailed confession; it was disgusting and horrible. He asked me if I thought he was going to hell. I told him that was between him and God.

Initiated by the Phoenix

Twenty-nine years later, Saturn returned to me a second time. To compare it to a hot mess would be an understatement. Saturn returned with the methodical Phoenix. Together they initiated me; I was left scorched. Paradise was burnt to ashes in one fatal day. My 16-year relationship was deteriorating, which left me dreaming of and feeling like the hanged woman in the tarot deck: upside down and waiting for this death cycle to end. I embraced painting as a spiritual practice. The grief was like a nagging dog at my ankles, the shadows rattling my nervous system. As a heart-centered Leo, I wanted to heal every single wound, including his. I did try. My attempts proved to be a tumultuous ride, with more heart-wrenching and powerful life-changing lessons.

On the day of the fire, I was in Hawaii with 30 other women and the artist Shiloh Sophia. We were celebrating and graduating together after the year-long intensive and life-changing "Color of Women" intentional creativity program. That morning, I got a call from my granddaughter asking where I was. She was crying, sharing with me that she was in traffic, escaping as she watched the town of Paradise, California, go up in flames. I soon received a call from my other granddaughter, who was trapped at Paradise High School. She asked me if I was okay. Later, firefighters rescued her. My son called next; he told me there were 50 mph winds. As he escaped the inferno, he saw my backyard on fire and knew we had lost our homes. The adrenaline was intense, the town was thick with black smoke, the wind and consuming flames created profuse explosions. The fire killed 85 people and destroyed 13,900 homes. Pets and wildlife were lost. It was over two months before we could return to see the remains of the inferno. I imagined the Phoenix screeching and flying overhead, our surrounding community consumed by thick, black smoke. Strangely, months before the fire, these words appeared in my dream: "It's hard not to see her in the bones and ashes of a rising Phoenix."

I was fortunate my daughter was living in Bali. I was able to visit her there and regulate my fragile nervous system as I approached what my intuitive nature knew was the breakdown of my marriage. There was so much shock happening after a tragedy of this magnitude. When I returned from Bali, most of Northern California was still consumed by toxic smoke. It literally took months for the fire to be extinguished and the smoke to clear. San Francisco airport was covered with a dark, ominous cloud. Schools were closed due to the ash that had built up hundreds of miles away. During the cycle of death and rebirth, I have discovered the Phoenix leaves imprints of her startling transformation far and wide.

Soul Embodiment

Since my initiation by the Phoenix, she has been an inspiration for my art. I have great respect for this mythical creature. I have painted various images of her. Intuitively, I painted to save my heart. My creativity included tree women, houses, keys, dream images, and archetypal guidance. As I painted Persephone, I was deeply aware of the parallel: feeling abducted and taken to the underworld of my marriage. I painted for my sanity in an attempt to understand what was happening and heal from the shock and trauma of losing everything that was familiar. I had become a nervous, confused mess, falling down the great abyss to the deep, dark underworld—the deepest, darkest night of my soul. My husband called me crazy when I confronted him. He denied and minimized his abusive behavior. On one occasion he yelled, "that's water under the bridge." I couldn't help but think, those were the very words my abusive grandfather spoke.

I dreamed of Bluebeard and he appeared in a painting, reiterating the abuse. The canvas was my portal, as I painted images from my shamanic journeys. After one particular abusive episode with my husband, I painted the archetype of Addie; "she who is addicted to abuse." After Addie, I painted my powerful self. I painted the Flower of Life, and many sacred symbols. Numerous paintings integrated pieces and fragments of my shattered heart. I painted to save my soul. My nervous system was dysregulated, and the reverberations jolted the deepest pain my heart had ever known. I realize now that the 50+ paintings and ten art journals I filled over the past three years have been my personal soul retrieval. With manifested purpose, I had been retrieving my dismembered soul parts. The tree women I had painted symbolized the deep roots of connection to the earth I had been longing for.

Alchemizing The Past

I became interested in the process of spiritual alchemy as I began to make sense of the seemingly uncontrollable changes in my life. Like the ancient alchemists, known for their intention of turning base metals into gold, spiritual alchemy is a system of bringing positive, lasting change. Spiritual alchemy can liberate us from our core wounds, transform core beliefs, restore lost soul parts, and alchemize self-destructive behavior. Once, during a shamanic journey, a guide told me, "Drugs are the medicine of the culture, to not feel ashamed of the past, of wanting to escape a bad situation or feeling the need to run away and numb the pain." Carl Jung taught us how to stop being our own saboteurs and allow our lives to unfold to their fullest potential.

I have discovered in the realm of spiritual alchemy that it is necessary to go through the stages of fire to get to the transformation of the Gold in life—the spiritual gold being self-actualization, contentment, harmony, and joy. Chaos, according to Jung, is the first stage of alchemy, associated with fire and burning off. The second stage—associated with water—is dissolution and is symbolized by intense emotions. Separation is the third stage, associated with the air element and freeing the self of resentments. Earth and the three previous elements make up the fourth stage, conjunction, and is synthesized as embodiment. The fifth stage, fermentation, corresponds with death of the old self and birth of the new—similar to the Phoenix rising from her own ashes.

The distillation phase brings together the shadow parts, or as Carl Jung would say, "making the unconscious conscious." Furthermore, he is quoted,

"Until you make the unconscious conscious, it will direct your life and you will call it fate." The final stage in spiritual alchemy is coagulation: becoming whole and healed. For example, recovering from a deep life altering wound.

"The Wind at Dawn Has Secrets to Tell You, Don't Go Back to Sleep."
—Rumi

In 2013 I began studying Shamanism. That year I invited a small circle of women to participate with me to share what I was taught. In Indigenous times, after a traumatic event, a shaman would call traumatized or lost soul parts back, in order for the individual to live integrated and whole. My friends and I began gathering on the various moon cycles. We experienced answers and insights for our collective group as we created a sacred container that stretched between the worlds of our circle. We continue to gather in ceremony on these auspicious days.

There is something that happens on a deep psychological level to want to go back and heal the wounds of the past. There is a slogan in twelve-step recovery: "Secrets keep you sick, and the truth will set you free." I have been on a mission to get to the truth. I remember initiating a shamanic journey with my husband. My guides told me he had a secret and the secret was revealed: he had relapsed. This began to explain the undisclosed nature of his behavior. I had been doing everything psychologically I could think of to heal our marriage. During couples therapy, I was told I have a high tolerance for abuse. Another couple's therapist told my husband he was a narcissist, going on to explain to him that he lacked empathy and compassion. As I sympathized with our plight, it did not change the situation. These realizations forced me to run.

An Old Era Is Ending

Science now proves that we can create new neural pathways and connections in our brain with the right interventions. We can also harm our brain with negative thoughts and harmful actions. Through healing arts, support, and education, I have embodied profound changes from these adversities. Nature has been a favorite restorative place. The wilds of Earth—especially places to be unplugged from the static frequencies—allow me to slow down to natural rhythms and disconnect from 5G and other invisible frequencies. A favorite practice is to ground myself to the Heart of Mother Earth by imagining my energy flowing deep to the core where her heart resides. There is a chart titled the Hertz Vibrational Scale. When I studied this chart, I realized that courage was the bridge to get from the lower vibrations of grief and anger to the higher vibrations I was longing for. I've had to be courageous in navigating an opponent who was once my lover and best friend.

I am getting into those higher frequencies as I continue to heal, using creativity as medicine. I have learned a great deal about grief and the nervous system. Some of my favorite healing practices are dancing, yoga, hiking, painting, Shamanism, women's circles, cold dips, music, EMDR, EFT tapping, nature, unplugging, grounding, crying, journaling, poetry, retreats, sisters, best friends, love, self-care, family, camping, kayaking, bicycling, meditating, ceremony, following the cycles of the moon, rituals, utilizing art as medicine, following like-minded women on social media, herbs such as ashwagandha, hawthorne, albizia, and medicinal mushrooms for my brain, theta music, flowers, healthy meals, creating ceramics, brain spotting, mindfulness, podcasts, affirmations, and twelve-step recovery. I always have tools at my fingertips and practices in my medicine basket.

Wild Woman

"It is worse to stay where one does not belong at all than to wander about lost for a while and looking for the psychic and soulful kinship one requires," says Clarissa Pinkola Estes, Ph.D. When I use the word "wild," I mean intuitive and wise. I learned this from Dr. Estes in her captivating book, Women Who Run With the Wolves. At the beginning of the pandemic, I facilitated a two-year virtual book club exploring these myths and stories of the Wild Woman archetype. She compares us to a wolf with a wild instinctual nature. What I concluded after reading this classic is that there was a predator. The predator can be a human, a creature, or a part of our own psyche—the predator demands unconsciousness.

My instinct led me to women artists who are steps ahead of me on this sacred creative path, and who have also contributed to Flower of Life Press.

I was in mentorship with Alexis Cohen before and after the fire. I was in the "Color of Women" with Shiloh Sophia before, during, and after the fire. I am mentoring with Whitney Freya. And I have mentored and danced with Sofiah Thom.

Intention

As I release this story, it is my sincere intention that it heals another layer in my ancestral lineage and the greater oneness of who we are as Human Beings. Courage is the bridge to the higher vibrations of love and joy. It is also part of my intention to release this glimpse of my life, into that etheric space in the quantum field to be transformed. Forever changed as medicine for the collective, witnessed as an experience of deep initiations that changed me into a stronger, more courageous Wild Woman. A lover who recognizes triggers, and no longer has a high tolerance for abuse. One who lovingly releases the old story and focuses on new trajectories. A future filled with loving awareness, courageous acts helping to heal the Collective Womb Wound in other Wild Women. One who lives life more in touch with her heart. Encircled by loving friends and part of the global community of soulful artists who are doing their part to raise the vibrational frequency of our Mother Earth. Standing at the threshold with a healed past, knowing each day is a new beginning.

Legend

I would like to share the Legend of the Red Thread. Those who were destined to meet are connected by an invisible Red Thread. I wear one tied to my wrist as a reminder that I am connected to something much larger than I can comprehend. So often I have felt overly responsible for others. There is the radical and liberating idea woven into this Legend, that I am only responsible for my piece. In circle, we pass the Red Thread as a reminder that we are all connected. I pass the Red Thread to you.

CHRISTINA MERCY, LCSW CHT RYT200 *passionately offers women creative practices to inspire their soul to greater healing. Combining years of training as a psychotherapist, she expresses herself as a deeply devoted practitioner of healing arts. She inspires women to uncover and mend psychological wounds. Her interest is in sharing her explorations of ancient, sacred and contemporary evidenced based studies. Assisting women in developing greater outcomes in their personal relationships with themselves, while supporting them in their deep soul work. Continuing her education, attaining certifications in yoga, Alchemical Hypnotherapy, Intentional Creativity, Temple Body Arts, and Creatively Fit coaching. She is a student of the esoteric wisdom traditions of shamanism, folk herbalism, meditation, and astrology. She is well versed in 12-step recovery. Christina conveys a deep passion and belief in the healing arts. Throughout her lifetime many teachers have shared wisdom and inspiration. She has integrated these lessons, and wove together guidance from her devotional spiritual practices and her soul's guidance. Her life has been a series of explorations. She incorporates Active Imagination, brought to us by the pioneer of depth psychology, Carl Jung. Her art practices incorporate the use*

of dream symbols, and archetypal images; as these can be sources of great information from our psyche. Dreams open the door to the vast reservoir of the collective unconsciousness. Her teaching includes the importance of intention and sacred ceremony, as she bravely embodies a curious and creative heart.

Learn more at **www.paintsinstardust.com**

InstaGram: *Christina Mercy paintsinstardust*

Facebook: *Evolving Soulful Women's Group* and *Christina Mercy Paints in Stardust*

FREE GIFT

My Gifts to You:

A Spotify Turning Point Play list: Christina Mercy Turning Point at Spotify.com

Free art class: Where did I come from? at paintsinstardust.com/offering

New Beginning Cake recipe at paintsinstardust.com/offering

"Saving My Heart" Cover Art by Christina Mercy
(for more details, see page xii)

CHAPTER 13

The Alchemy of Dying in Your Dreams

Messages From the Other Side

By Ericha Scott, PhD, LPCC, ATR-BC, REAT

"Owning the shadow involves confronting it and assimilating its contents into an enlarged self-concept. Such healing encounters typically occur in midlife, but meetings with the shadow can happen whenever we feel life stagnate and lose its color and meaning. Especially when we recognize and feel the constricting effects of denial, or when we doubt the values we live by and watch our illusions about ourselves and the world shatter, or when we are overcome by envy, jealousy, sexual drives, or ambition, or feel the hollowness of our convictions—then shadow-work can begin."

—Meeting the Shadow: The Hidden Power of the Dark Side of Human Nature, *edited by Connie Zweig and Jeremiah Abrams*

Leaving Texas at age six, I sat in the back seat of the car and sang the refrain from "Remember the Alamo" through most of Oklahoma. I sang softly until my mother told me to be quiet.

By the age of nine, I had lived in three states. Although I lived an upper-middle-class lifestyle, I felt cast adrift and lost. My father, grandparents, aunts and uncles, cousins, teachers, and friends all lived elsewhere. In hindsight, it is not a surprise to me that I would dream about feeling lost on a highway without a clear idea of where I was going. What was a surprise—a frightening shock, really—was to dream about helplessly, senselessly, and realistically dying in a dream.

Death Dream I: End of First Semester, My Senior Year of College

I thought, "This is a stupid way to die."

Touching my throat, I could feel the sticky blood pulsing from the wound in my neck.

I knew I only had a few minutes left, as my consciousness faded into black. Then I woke up. I woke up terrified and in shock because I did not think someone could die in a dream.

During my last year of college, twice in six months, I dreamed that I died.

My mother told me that I had nearly died in surgery before the age of five. This has always felt right to me, even though anesthesia had blurred these memories.

Fortunately, I have kept a dream journal since middle school. This offered me the opportunity to remember and observe the experiences and meanings of my life and dreams as they unfolded in depth and breadth over time.

I have realized that new meanings do not cancel out old interpretations. Both interpretations can be true, even if they seem paradoxical. The etiology of dreams is multi-causal and the meanings can be multidimensional.

I have also come to realize that my nightmares are just as important and healing as my overtly beautiful, luminescent, and transcendent spiritual dreams.

If I designed a t-shirt slogan about this concept, it would be, "Nightmares are My Friends."

For over 50 years, I have recorded, processed, and illustrated my dreams in a variety of ways, including poetry, writing, photography, and painting. In the following pages, I share the content of two life-changing dreams. Although the dreams are quite different, both contributed in tandem to a major turning point in my life.

At the beginning of the first dream, a nightmare, I was driving alone on an empty highway.

I was lost in Tennessee, the land of my ancestors, while searching for a gas station. I needed gas and directions.

Still lost, I turned off the highway onto a lonely country road. I hoped I would find better luck on a narrow road than the wide highway.

This road was lined by trees with a creek on one side and a ditch with farmland on the other. It was beautiful and yet also deserted. I could not see anyone anywhere.

The further I drove, the more helpless and frustrated I felt. I was going nowhere.

Finally, the road ended at a cul-de-sac. At the very top of the circle was a two story, white, clapboard house. The house was set far back from the road, and it was being renovated.

I pulled up to the curb, leaned over the passenger seat, rolled down my window, and asked two strange men for directions. One was short and the other was tall and yet they looked like brothers. They both answered me differently at the same time. They were not speaking in unison. Their directions sounded garbled and confusing. I could not hear one over the other.

I knew I needed help and somehow the help they offered was not helpful.

I asked them to repeat themselves, one at a time, when suddenly, as if by magic, they were sitting inside my car.

This was extremely uncomfortable. I had not unlocked the car doors, nor I had not invited them to join me, and these grown men were much older and larger. I wondered, "How did they get inside my car?"

In real life, I was only 24 years old, and I weighed about 90 pounds.

One of the two men was sitting in my driver's seat. I had been displaced and reduced. The other man was sitting in the front passenger's seat. I was in the back seat behind the passenger. I found myself sitting next to a petite old lady who had silver white hair pulled back into a bun. I felt as if I should know her, but I could not place her identity, in the dream or in my life. Now, when I think of her, I realize that more than anyone else, she looks like me as I do today over forty years later.

She was marveling about how young I looked for my age. The two men, her sons, agreed. This conversation did not feel like a compliment. They were discussing, as if I was not present, how I looked way too young. They kept repeating themselves. I was silent and confused.

I thought, "What does my age or appearance have to do with directions, or a map, or the fact that I am lost?"

Suddenly, the man in the driver's seat turned, leaned forward, and pointed a gun at me. He said in a menacing voice, "You just look too young to live!" Before I could move or react, he pulled the trigger. I felt the full force of the bullet's impact. I could smell gunpowder. I touched the center of my wounded neck and felt wet, warm, and sticky blood pulsing out of my body. Immediately, I knew I was dying. I thought, "WHY? WHY NOW? WHAT A STUPID WAY TO DIE!"

Quickly, I lost blood and consciousness in the dream. After dying, I woke up.

The content and the sensations of this nightmare did not leave me for weeks. I could not shake off the quality of dread, futility, and foreboding I had felt. The somatic feelings from my nightmare globalized and in more conscious way, became associated with my life.

I talked about this dream, over and over, with my friends and teachers. I processed this dream in every way I could imagine. I thought about it as I walked around a large lake. I wrote it out in detail. I identified and recognized much of the symbology and even whom the dream figures might represent.

Finally, I decided that like the dream, I was lost and wandering aimlessly in life without any direction. Asking my family for useful guidance was taking me down the wrong pathway. Just like the dream, the help they offered was not helpful. After giving it a lot of thought, I realized that I had a sense of purposelessness and foreboding about my life that the dream was communicating to me.

Fortunately, I realized that what I could change was my own motivation. In other words, I owned my shadow. The next semester, my last semester, I actually read the class textbooks and completed the assignments. I studied and prepared for tests. My mid-range B average jumped to all A's and one B. In fact, in my business class, I ruined the curve. Because I listened to my dream imagery as a link to my subconscious mind, I felt propelled to a higher level of academic achievement. Fortunately, the dead-end cul-de-sac in the nightmare prevented a potential dead-end for my young life.

Death Dream 2: 6 Months Later, Just A Few Weeks After Graduation

I stared at my professor. I could see his lips moving, I could hear what he was saying, and I could see tears in his eyes, but who died? Bobby? Bobby who? I was in shock.

I was not connecting the dots.

I had just seen Bobby the day before.

I could not make any sense of it. Confused I said, "I don't know who you are talking about, 'Who is Bobby?'" My professor looked at me with surprise and concern, "Bobby, your friend, your friend in art class. It was on the news this morning. He died in a car crash."

The next few days were a blur. A few days later, during a weekend nap, once again I dreamed about dying. In simplistic terms, I died in my dream to meet Bobby in the Bardo.

In the summer of 1977, I had just graduated from college. For a few months, I worked as a waitress. During that time of transition, even though I had significantly raised my GPA the last few months of school, I continued to carry a sense of restlessness, self-doubt, and questions about the direction of my future. For example, "How was I going to support myself as an artist?"

One week, I was asked to come to the country club to work for a luncheon event. It was the first and last time I was in the country club to work during the day.

As I previously mentioned, Bobby had also been an art student. He and I were both friends with our art teacher, and sometimes the three of us would go out to a local bar after class. Although friends, I had not seen Bobby for months, since long before our graduation.

The afternoon I worked, I happened to be standing where I could see the front door when Bobby walked into the club. He and I were both surprised to, almost literally, run into each other. He was wearing a uniform and it took me a minute to recognize him, and it took him a few moments to recognize me as well. It was a very warm and sweet surprise.

What transpired over the next few days, the tragedy of his sudden death and the dream visitation that followed imprinted a somatic and sensory experience of love that I can still feel to this day.

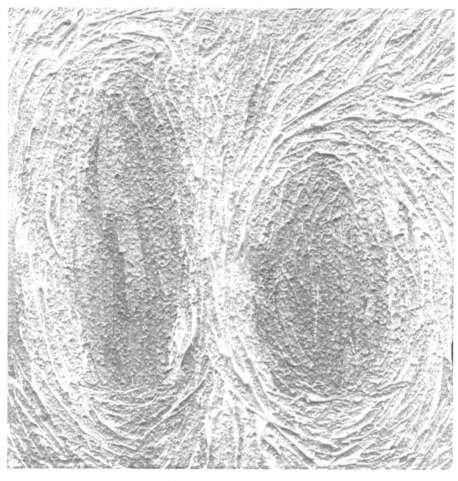

"Bobby in the Bardo" by Ericha Scott

WHAT WE CANNOT SEE

Fog is like a lace, silk slip
worn by a beautiful woman.

The lace directs and focuses
our attention, to what we know exists,
to what can be seen and what is unseen.

Fog flows, mutates, and changes beauty,
for better or worse.

My soul is comforted.

I have heard it said, "Fog is the breath of God."

Is it possible to be spiritually
seduced, in a way that is holy?

Have deviant cults
and corrupt religious leaders,
ruined that
for us all?

I know this...
It is OKAY to be mysterious in an era
of harsh lights.

There is no need for a flash or strobe lights
that make people blink and wince.

I could not understand why people lived
in the northwestern United States, until
I arrived in time to see
a brightly colored totem pole
slowly emerge from inside of a cloud.

Too many facts, too much fiction,
too many pills, booze, and sex
numb us, distort our perceptions,
and defeat us.

I saw you that morning, a black silhouette
at the top of the stairs,

framed by the arched doorway,
under a liminal,
in an un-sacred space, surrounded by a luminous
halo of Florida's blinding, hot, summer sun.

I was not supposed to be there,
you weren't either.

The restaurant was flooded
with streamers of light stretching
across a musky forever.

I did not recognize you at first.
A new haircut, a new uniform,
you had lost weight, and your
hand cart was loaded with beer.

I feel so fortunate.
I got to hug you the day you died,
in a fire storm, a head on car crash.

I took a nap the next weekend,
exhausted by shock and denial.

A few of your fraternity brothers
arrived at work
to warn me
in dreamtime.
I found it amusing,
Big American guys, so afraid

because they had seen you after death.

I scoffed, "I am not afraid of Bobby's ghost!"
UNSAID: "Don't waste my time."

Until I saw an exact likeness
of you walking toward me in perfect
photorealistic focus, and slightly off,
and it was not a ghost.
It was not you.
The likeness was completely empty,
a void filled with nothingness.

I cried out, "It looks like him, it looks like him,
but that is not him!"

"That's NOT Bobby!"

I repeated this to myself over and over.

I could see
the frat boys try to catch me
as I swooned,
their faces concerned, hovering.

Dizzy, I tumbled, fainted,
and died.

Once again, I thought, "Can I die in a dream?"
I continued to fall
through concrete
and asphalt.

Into the middle of what was
dense and gray.

I stood alone, in silence, disoriented.
There was nothing under my feet.
Suspended in time and space.

I waited
disappointed.

I asked myself, "If this is heaven, where is the color?"

I searched and saw
two vertical, oblong shadows take form.

I recognize you right away. Elated, I waved and
called out your name with excitement and joy!

You approach and I begin to feel your love
saturate me
down to my blood and bones,
cells and neurons.

You envelop me with a love
I have never felt before or since.
I want to let go and fade into
THIS form of nothingness except love.
I rest here.

Gently, you tell me that I do not have to go back.

I lean back. "WHAT?"

You say again, "You do not have to go back."
"You can stay here."

I feel and hear myself sigh aloud in my sleep.

I look to my left at your tall, skinny guide.
He does not move, nor does he protest.

I turn my focus back to you.

"Bobby, I must go back. I do not know why.
There is something I must do.
I don't know what it is."

You release me as I gently pull away,
Slowly I wake up from a dream,
if it was a dream,
to try, in my humble and inadequate way,
to create a better world.

© 12/09—12/17/21

I grew up in a southern home full of niceties and hate. Rarely did I see an expression of love that held congruent integrity.

Feeling saturated by the sensations of love in my dream, without someone trying to take something away from me, was novel, and it changed me. Bobby, my friend and dream figure, gave me a dream-time physical sensation and imprint of love. This love became a bright, red north star to guide me.

In some ways I consider this dream to have been a spiritual intervention.

It took a while, almost a decade, for me to turn around the ship of my life and aim it in the right direction.

In hindsight, it is not ironic that I have designed educational art projects and led custom-designed therapeutic workshops about nightmares, trauma resolution, ego-states, dissociation, addiction, holistic health, interfaith spirituality, poetry, art psychotherapy, and love letters for the last 38 years or more.

If you want to enrich your life and enhance your creativity, I encourage you to keep a dream journal. The right way to keep a dream journal is YOUR way of keeping a dream journal. Please fill your journal with images, collages, words, dialogue, and how these correlate with your life. Also, please remember this: you are the expert on the meaning of your symbols and metaphors.

My personal axiom is, "People have more grief over unexpressed love than profound trauma. Tell people you love them."

I invite you to join me on this journey of embracing creativity and love more deeply to better connect with yourself, others, and the divine.

FREE GIFT

My Gift to You:

Haiku Poetry—A handout description of how to write a Haiku Poem.

To access, visit **www.artspeaksoutloud.org**

ERICHA SCOTT, PHD, LPCC, ATR-BC, REAT

For thirty-eight years, Dr. Scott has been a healer who walks the fine line between mysticism and evidenced-based psychotherapy. She is a Licensed Clinical Professional Counselor (LPCC917) in California and she is certified as an interfaith spiritual director, Reiki master, addiction counselor, and dually certified creative and expressive arts therapist. She is an international bestselling author, artist, poet, and keynote speaker.

Dr. Scott is also a fellow for the oldest trauma organization in the world, The International Society for the Study of Trauma and Dissociation, and is an expert in grief, trauma, dissociation, self-harm, nightmares, integrative health, and the creative arts psychotherapies.

She designed and facilitated art psycho-educational and creative arts therapeutic workshops for almost four decades and has been recognized throughout the United States and abroad for her original, unique, and powerful healing experiences.

Dr. Scott's academic writing and research have been published in trade magazines, textbooks, and peer-review journals by The Journal of Chemical Dependency, UCLA, Oxford University Press, Taylor and Francis, and others.

Dr. Scott is accepting clients for 2-5 day private, individual, and custom-designed creative arts intensives.

*To learn more, please visit her website at **www.artspeaksoutloud.org**. To book her as a speaker, retreat leader, or for a creative and expressive arts intensive, please contact her directly at 310-880-9761.*

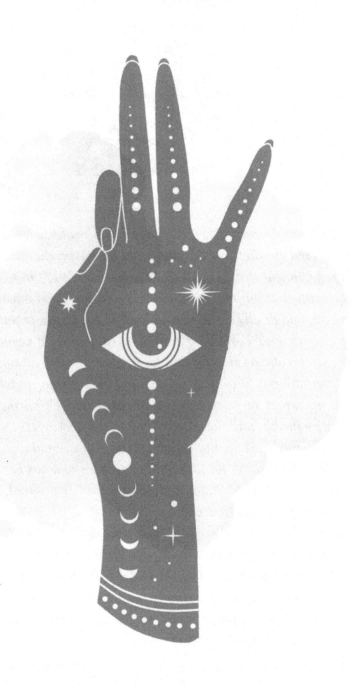

CHAPTER 14

Celebrate the Fall

My Mythic Journey Home

By Judith Snyder

> *"The wound is the place where the light enters you."*
> —Rumi

I was a sensual child, immersed in the magic of nature. I could not have been more than two years old when I saw that sweet blade of grass wrapped in dew. My body shimmered to a silent rhythm that tickled my skin and fluttered my heart like delicate butterfly wings—the entire cosmos was dancing in me. I had a similar experience when, at three years old, I walked by the pink rose bush planted in my childhood home; her petals soaking through my pores, her essence filling my body with sweet nectar. Of course, I did not understand these concepts then. It was not until my late twenties—my first Saturn Return—when I discovered that nature, *the earth,* was my safe haven; my deep connection to the *divine feminine*—the place where I would slowly re-member who I *truly* am; where that constant ache of brokenness would subside, and I would feel held in a nourishing chrysalis.

My first true lesson with Rose unraveled when I was seven years old, during a visit to my grandmother's home. She was my mother's mother; a sweet, nurturing woman whose inner resilience and fortitude cradled me in a fierce love that was deeply grounding to my soul. She, like my mother, was birthed through the lineage of the Sacred Rose, and she grew the most magical rose bush in her garden. I visited this rose bush regularly. But on that particular visit, as I reached for her petals, I lost my footing and fell straight into her velvety flowers AND prickly stems.

It was here that I met Thorn in all her glory and pain. I ran toward my mother for comfort with a tear-stained face. My mother's eyes, however, were vacant, as depression had overtaken her ability to tend to my wounded body and broken heart. And my father? Well, he was traumatized in battle during WWII. It was my Auntie Irene who would tend to me then. And my godparents. They were like fairy angels who took me on regular visits to our community rose gardens. We would visit each family of roses, their vibrant colors immersing us in their magnificence. I often wondered how my godparents knew my heart longed to feel close to these beautiful beings. Perhaps it was my mother who told them, or perhaps it was simply divine grace. Whoever or whatever it was knew the importance of having these moments etched into my heart.

One day, in 6th grade, while learning about planets in science class, I suddenly encountered my first out-of-body experience. I was terrified. It was as if my essence left my body in one fell swoop, and a plethora of sensory data flooded my psyche. With every cell in my body hypersensitized, each day became a grave effort to manage. My twelve-year-old self felt as if an intense earthquake uprooted my body, ripping out my limbs, bit by bit. Hence, my first full-blown 'panic attack' was born. This abruptly *awakened* my parents as they diligently searched for a therapist to support me. I felt fully seen and held by them for the very first time. Although, because of our culture's over-focus on quick fixes, diagnosing, and medication, I became the 'problem child' and my deep shame imprints—*There's something wrong with me!* and *I must be crazy!*—were rapidly ignited. It would be over two decades before I became more acquainted with my multidimensionality and realized that what my twelve-year-old self was *really* experiencing was my first spiritual awakening and ancient embodied memory. My entire human journey since has been to deepen my understanding of this encounter with the *other realms* and with my sacred mission to rewrite our *her*story through the mythical journey of the soul.

During my early teens, I budded into my wild self, my sacred sexuality coming online as my body vibrated to a whole new ecstatic rhythm. I loved to go on radical adventures, birthing a new, or shall I say *ancient,* aspect of myself that felt quite unfamiliar. I longed to shake up the status quo; to share openly about how I felt, especially around those I saw as harming the vulnerable. The authentic power that took root in me felt fiery as I began to stand my ground for what I believed in and to support others in doing the same. Our culture at that time was deeply imbued in the message that children are to be seen and not heard, so to have a voice and express your truth was profoundly provocative and quickly dismissed. As my wildness began to take root and take flight, the chaos within my family accentuated, and I could feel the crumbling of whatever support was left. And that beautiful sacred primal energy? Well, it was externalized through my first intimate encounter with boys and alcohol since my sense of self was not yet strong enough. These encounters would become deeply initiatory; at first, they offered a place of inner safety. Of peace. Of belonging. Over time, however, they began to peel away layers of my sense of self-worth—very subtly and very cunningly. Still, the theme of men and alcohol was very much alive in me until my first Saturn Return at 28. By that time, cocaine had also become my lover.

Cocaine quickly jump-started my downward spiral into the Underworld—the place some of us call the Dark Night of the Soul. It had its rotting tentacles hooked inside me. So much so that I believed with my entire being that it was saving my life…saving my life from a cycle of unending shame and pain. It gave me a deep sense of courage, strength, and confidence, and all semblance of fear seemed to quickly dissipate. Until it no longer did. I began to make choices that severed me, cutting me off more and more deeply from my body's innate wisdom. I was numb to myself, numb to others, numb to life. I wanted to die.

But instead, I was cradled by divine grace. It was a Sunday morning following another weekend binge when my phone rang as I stepped out of the shower. Under 'normal' circumstances in my deluge of depression, I would not have answered it. But on this particular day, I did. On the other end was the voice of my elder sister, who, at the time, worked at a drug and alcohol rehab center. She had heard of my demise from my other sister and mother, who were sick with worry. She shared some truths about alcoholism; that it was a 'dis-ease of feelings,' not of uncontrollable drinking. And what she shared, along with the deep compassion that poured through the phone, allowed my body to soften, to let go, to be held. This was on May 1st, 1988, on Beltane; the day I laid down my last drink and drug by the grace of God*dess*.

A few days later, I was off to a 28-day program—what I now call, 'Inner Sanctuary.' It changed my life and opened me up to my spiritual path and to my first great Turning Point. It was in this protective space that I began to heal layers of heartache. It was where I first learned the meaning of 'hugs not drugs,' and where vulnerable sharing opened me up to true intimacy. I began to let others penetrate the hard shell I had created years earlier. Men, who I had deeply mistrusted, I now witnessed breaking down as they shared their loss of control of alcohol, losing their families, homes, friends, and jobs. I learned about spirituality and creative expression, watching people transform their lives while others lost hope and returned to the thralls of alcohol. It was a slow process as my emotions reawakened, feeling and releasing deeply held grief and rage—my innocence had been ripped away at a young age while being silenced time and time again. I learned that by sharing my truth, I was also helping others to heal. Over time, my trust was restored. When I completed my stay at the sanctuary, my entire experience was wrapped into one heartfelt memory: a circle of us gathered around a grand piano singing Amazing Grace. To this day, I am deeply moved by this memory and this most sacred song.

My spiritual path continued to blossom as I became deeply connected to paganism and other earth-based forms of spirituality. I remembered my love of nature, ceremony, and ritual; of honoring my ancestors and the earth. I opened up to the world of essential oils and flower essences, sipping them into my cells where my wounds continued to heal. Guided to yoga, I remembered my love of the body, and of creating sacred movement aligned with devotion to inner listening, to my sensuality, and to the cycles of nature. I was invited to Glastonbury for their annual Goddess Conference, where I remembered my ancient priestess roots, where the land welcomed my homecoming, and where the Mists of Avalon sang to my soul. I felt renewed and realigned with my sacred mission to help others remember their inner truth and creative self-expression.

The aspect of myself that had taken root in me as a teen, I was now ready to integrate through the wisdom I had gained. I began to feel grounded and whole; a spaciousness I had not felt since my early childhood days while spending time with the roses. I was trained as a *SOMA*tic licensed therapist with a specialty in the impact of trauma on the body. I helped my clients release their trauma through reconnecting with their divine feminine, listening deeply into their bodies to hear and honor their soul. And as those of us along this spiritual path know, we as healers and guides are initiated deeper into these realms so that our gifts are purified and potentized. So in again I went, though unaware of the depth of heart wounds that lay there, aching to be healed…and soon to be revealed.

I was in my mid-forties when I was ready to share my life with someone. After all, I had worked through many layers of pain and grief. I even drew an oracle card that indicated the timing was ripe for an intimate relationship. So, when I received a message out of the blue from a dear friend whose name contained the word *rose* and who wanted me to meet a colleague of hers, I believed this was surely a 'match made in heaven' and that he and I were destined to be together. He had a Ph.D. in psychology, which, in my mind, sealed the deal. We would have a mutual desire to be of service and would both work on ourselves and our relationship. This is not how it unfolded. We did experience the usual triggers and were determined to deepen our intimacy, working hard at honest communication and transparency. We did share openly about our fears and distrust. After some time, however, I noticed that something felt off about him. His anger would often feel unprovoked. My body began giving me cues of potential danger, though I ignored her time and time again, wanting to work through layers of resistance and believing I just needed to try harder. The anger episodes seemed few and far between, though their increasing intensity was apparent. My body was giving me countless messages that said, *I don't feel safe,* but there was a part of me that believed I could fix him. After all, I was a licensed therapist.

We moved in together. After an initial honeymoon period, our arguments and triggers intensified. I was not yet ready to go deep into my pain and own my part to at least help decrease the possibility of things escalating. I was still sorting through what was mine and what was not. And then, following one very intense argument, his anger was triggered and quickly escalated to uncontrollable rage; the kind that unleashes undeniable terror, similar to how I felt as a child during my father's rage—numb, shamed, and silenced. The next thing I remember is being dragged out of our bedroom and down the hall. I then remember the deep primal part of me kicking in and thinking to myself, *you will never knock me down. My integrity is intact.* Then, out of nowhere, my cat appeared. I quickly scooped her up and pressed her to my heart. I then felt a jolt behind me (he later said he pushed me, not with the intention of pushing me down that half-flight of stairs, but to scare me). As my body thrust forward, and I braced myself for the impending impact, my cat flew out of my arms and tumbled down the stairs. Thank Good*dess* she was unharmed, at least physically. This was the moment my *Warrioress* energy flooded my body, and I knew within myself that something would need to change. I called the police. He was told to leave for the night. This felt like justice.

Even though this experience scarred me, I stayed. I stayed and agreed to couples therapy. We were married and continued therapy for the remainder of our five years together. The physical altercations stopped, but during a particularly stressful time, the final and worst one was triggered. I left for good, never looking back. At the same time, I was filled with shame. *How did this happen? I should know better, I'm a therapist, and I've done so much healing.* Still, part of me knew that this experience humbled me and prepared me to be of service to other women while opening deep wounds so I could heal. I later understood that this experience occurred during my Chiron Return and that I was healing wounds not just from childhood but from other lifetimes and dimensions. This was my second great Turning Point—I was now more at peace.

At this point, I was ready to *slow down* and listen even more deeply to my body—this vast vessel of star sparkles creating entire universes within; portals to the divine. I began to hear the trees, the flowers, and the animals communicate. I thought everyone could feel these vibrations until I was ready to hear that this was my unique gift; that I had a deep connection with Gaia's sacred language. That I could sense her rhythm and a deep sense of oneness with the cosmos. That those childhood moments with Rose, Thorn, and that sweet blade of grass were the harmony by which the divine communicated with me. That my body knew how to move energy to create beauty, even—and especially—the vibration of 'shadows.' I drew in cosmologies and teachers that helped me ground and contain these experiences, such as Human Design, Gene Keys, Stellar Nations, Animism, and Light Language. These cosmologies entered my life during my 2nd Saturn Return and became my next series of initiations, my final great Turning Point as of this writing.

As I step into my elder years, I find myself back in a deep dark womb space. I have been here for some time. I feel the intricacy of Life here. While a part of me would love to stay in this familiar invisible space, I feel myself being pulled upward, as if the sun were pouring its magnificent light into my being, longing to feel my blossoms. I am guided to expand my mission around death; to help souls find their way once they have surrendered their physical bodies. As I play with this energy, I am moved by the deaths I have experienced in this lifetime; beautiful deaths that have broken my heart open. My father, mother, and sister were among them, each of whom I deeply grieved, and with each, a portal opened into the mystery and wonder of death—my fears commanding their rightful place as well.

Through the death of my beloved cat, Miwa, in 2019, I felt this even more succinctly. As she awoke me early one October morning, I was initiated into the embodied celebration of dancing through the realms of death. My hands reached for her body as she fell to the floor, and as we danced, she died in my arms. In my shock and grief, I could not say how far into these realms we danced, but I knew in those moments that her death was a ceremonial initiation. I wrapped her body in a tapestry-laced scarf and covered her in pink rose petals, crystals, and a thousand sacred tears. Again, I remembered the wisdom I had gained as a child from Rose, Thorn, and that sweet blade of grass wrapped in dew, forever mirroring their exquisite beauty in the never-ending cycles of birth, death and rebirth.

We have all gone through an enormous planetary shift. Many of us are still finding our way to a new grounding, some of which is quite taxing on our physical bodies. Through this process, we are lovingly held by Gaia. She is tending to us. Nourishing us in her rich, *dark,* fertile soil. Her magic weaves within us the vibrations of our own unique soul song. *And we are remembering.*

As we continue our journey into the Great Mystery, may we always remember that we are divine sparkles of light, that our wounds are sacred ground, that our scars are ancient and holy, that we are never ever alone... And may we always remember to dance!

FREE GIFT

My Gift to You:

'Mystical Dance in the Forest' embodiment audio + free 30 minute session

This embodiment audio is a mystical journey into a magical forest where you are invited to deepen into the presence of your soul through the sacred mirror of nature and remember your love of shadows and light. There, you ignite the beauty of your e-motions as vibrant expressions of your authentic sovereignty. After, you are offered a free 30-minute session, where you have the opportunity to share your intentions, desires, and challenges.

To access, visit **dancingindelight.com/product/mystical-dance-in-the-forest/**

JUDITH SNYDER *is a light dancer, myth weaver, so-journ guide, and SOMAtic therapist. Her love of the body's innate wildness and intuitive intelligence has guided her along her path, opening her heart to* The Sacred *in all cycles of the human journey; birth, death and rebirth. Since childhood, she has felt a deep sensitivity for humanity and the earth, and assisted others for over three and a half decades in reclaiming their sovereignty through celebrating their shadows.*

Judith lives in a quaint town nestled within the Pocono Mountains of Northeastern Pennsylvania where she continues to dance with nature and help women re-create their life experiences through the mythic eyes of the soul.

Connect with her work and subscribe to her newsletters at **www.dancingindelight.com**

CHAPTER 15

Nature, Art, and Love Synthesize in Wholeness

By Crystal L. Steinberg

The night after my mother died, a Luna moth appeared at our window four nights in a row. She persistently beat her wings against the glass. I never saw such a moth flying freely in nature. I wondered about the pattern of returning each night, but we needed to make funeral arrangements, so I simply noted her presence. As I spoke on the phone with a friend during the fourth night, I told her about the moth and placed my hand on the windowpane where she again hovered. This time she clung to the window and stopped flapping her wings. Our energy connected through the glass for half an hour before she flew away, never to return.

Luna moths live only a short, seven- to ten-day adult life span. During this time, they must find a mate, procreate, and lay hundreds of eggs for their species' life cycle to continue. Why had this moth chosen to spend such a significant portion of her adult life with me? When I shared the story with my spiritual director, she asked, "Did you investigate the spiritual significance of a Luna moth?"

The first sentence of my search read, "A visiting Luna moth is thought to contain the soul of a loved one." My heart leaped for joy. Could it be that my mother came to assure me that she was okay? That the energy so palpable through the glass meant that everything is energy and that transitions are only transformations of form? As I continued reading, the lifecycle became a numeric metaphor for my mother's life: seven days for the eggs to hatch, eight weeks in the larval phase, and nine months in the pupa phase. Nine months isolated with imaginal cells bearing the gift of winged light in the unknown shadows of darkness. Almost an entire life spent on one significant, mysterious transformation with a short time to share its beauty and wisdom.

When my mom received her terminal diagnosis, she was given nine months to two years to live. She died nine months later. Those nine months contained a mysterious transformation where she shared her love and beauty. This had not always been the case. My parents and I, like many of us, shared a contentious relationship. My father left when I was a toddler. He was the love of my mother's life, and his leaving nearly destroyed her. It separated her from her highest creative and artistic self. She declined an art school scholarship to marry him and then, after my sister and I were born, he left.

Mesmerized by her unfinished canvases and oil paints in the fruit cellar, I longed to learn how to create at my mother's knee, but she could not be found at the easel. I mourned her absence there. Even as a child, something inside me knew that creativity was our connection. But work, childcare, survival needs, and finding a second husband took precedence. Unfortunately, as is so often the case, the second husband turned out to be a predator. When my mom finally decided to leave him, he fought her for six tortuous years.

This left me in a caretaking role as my mom's physical health declined. At that time, I was the only caretaker available. I never fully satisfied all her needs. I became aware of this when she hired Rent-A-Daughter to fill in the gaps left by my child-raising, full time teaching, and marriage. We spent years processing our anger. I was angry with her for keeping my sister and me in harm's way for so long after learning about her second husband's abuse. She was angry at me for not satisfying all her needs, which I simply couldn't do.

Eventually, art opened a portal of growing forgiveness. Having designed a "Literature and Visual Arts" curriculum, the Art Institute of Chicago hired me as a consultant. My students and I taught high school teachers how we used gallery exhibits to inform our reading, writing, and creating. This work allowed me to enter the museum before hours and remain afterward. When I traveled to the Institute to prepare units, my mom often accompanied me. She started sketching again while I worked. We enjoyed conversations about art together during lunch and after hours; she showed me what new discoveries she found in the museum that day. It was not long until she started to take art classes and bring some of these sketches into her work.

Marlene's hand-drawn abstract

By the time she received the terminal diagnosis, I saw my role as facilitating her living as she was actively dying. We shared so many wonderful conversations and experiences as we spoke each day and traveled, if chemo brain and fatigue did not get the best of her. I still remember the delighted smile on her face during the encore of a performance of a Million Dollar Quartet. She stood, clapping her hands and singing the Jerry Lee Lewis, Johnny Cash, and Carl Perkins songs with the rest of the audience. We sat in front of Picasso's series of 11 lithographs depicting the spirit of a bull equaling its form for over an hour as she explained why she would order them differently. We dined in the old Marshall Field's Walnut room, where dustings by the fairies there kept a twinkle in her eyes.

The day before she died, we had just returned from a trip to Hawaii that my mom gifted her family after refusing to be part of a clinical cancer trial.

While we waited outside the airport for the shuttle to our car, I asked her, "Are you sure you don't want to go for your blood counts? We stayed an extra week."

"No, I just want to get home and sleep in my own bed."

"Do you want me to stay?"

"No, you kids need some rest, too. Go home and we'll get the blood counts tomorrow."

Something inside me told me to stay anyway, but my body did need rest after the long trip home. I convinced myself that I would be of more help to her the next day if I slept in my own bed. She would probably be admitted for transfusions and that also required the energy to keep her spirits up. I'd wheel her through the peace garden, and we might sketch a bit. The walks on the cancer floor were the most difficult. They included passing the children's rooms where my mom would always say, "Now that's not fair. I got to live my life and they aren't getting to live theirs." This made mom into a passionate St. Jude's hospital contributor. We continue contributing in this spirit and in her name.

But I didn't sleep well in my own bed. I dreamt that my mom fell and died. It felt like I was fighting to wake up and help, but I couldn't. I kept realizing things that were left undone and would now fall to me. Things we had discussed, and that she had not finalized decisions about. We thought we had more time. We returned from the trip to prepare for months of transfusions and a bedside vigil.

When my mom called the next morning feeling lightheaded and asking me to come and drive her to the hospital for blood counts, I was already up and packing a bag for the hospital. Not knowing what we would find, I was bringing anything I might need for a few days stay: nutritious food rather than vending machine offerings, a comfy change of clothes in case I needed to stay overnight, a journal, and art materials to co-create with the plants and flowers in the Peace Garden. "I'm just about ready to walk out the door," I assured her.

"Thank you. I am so grateful for you, and I love you so much." These were the last words I ever heard my mom speak to me. How fortunate for us that in the normal exchanges generated in the path of healing our relationship and her terminal diagnosis, we had developed such habits.

The next call I received once on my way came from one of my mom's senior housing neighbors. "Your mom has fallen and doesn't seem right."

"Call an ambulance and don't move her!" I shouted.

"We already moved her into a chair."

"Okay, can you stay there until I get there? I'm about 15 minutes away." I hoped that my mom fell because she was lightheaded and nothing more. By the time I arrived, the paramedics were pulling up. When I entered my mom's apartment, she seemed like she was sleeping with her head to one side. There didn't appear to be any evidence of her head hitting anything. No blood on the carpet, no bleeding from her head, but she wasn't speaking, just nodding her head in response to questions.

While she was examined, I went to retrieve the doctor's information about her condition to show the team. Not finding any physical explanation for her lack of speech, the paramedics decided to transport her for a blood transfusion. They asked me to meet them at the hospital. Fifteen minutes into the half-hour transport, the paramedics interrupted my call, explaining things to my husband. They reported an emergency need to reroute to the nearest hospital because my mom started seizing.

When we reunited in the ER, the doctor told me they suspected my mom had a cranial bleed from the fall and didn't have much time left. As these words left the doctor's mouth, my mom began seizing. My first instinct was to hold her shaking body. "I'm here, I'm here," I whispered in her ear. She stopped seizing. "Do you want me to call Chris?" her beloved grandson who lived a distance away. He and her great-grandson came to spend a week in Hawaii with us but could not remain the additional week mom decided to stay.

Fortunately, we had a layover in the airport nearest his home on the way back. Our families gathered for a meal. I remember noticing how my mom seemed to be looking at each one of us, moving her head in slow motion as if it was for the last time; the smile on her great-grandson's face when she gifted him a pen from the Oceanarium he didn't have a chance to visit; laughing and joking about the trip. A sort of Last Supper unbeknown to us. Hugs and kisses for the trip home. Mom held my hand the entire flight. Her biggest fear about traveling was that she would die somewhere along the way and complicate getting home. She was grateful to be on the last leg of this particular journey.

Tears fell from her eyes as he spoke to her through my phone. I do not know what he said, but I watched my mom's head move up and down. It was a deep connection. Nine years later he still wears one of the purple bands we had printed when mom was diagnosed that reads, *Praying for Marlene and everyone with cancer.*

She started seizing again and I took the phone saying, "I'll call you as soon as I can." Beeping machines announced a team of medical personnel.

"We don't think we can get a scan with her seizing like this, so we're going to assume that she has a cranial bleed."

"What does that mean in terms of time?" I asked, not wanting to know the answer.

"At most a couple of hours," the doctor reported.

Mom seized again. I held her once more, this time saying, "Look for grandma and grandpa. They'll show you the way."

"Do you want me to get the chaplain for you?" the doctor asked. "You really shouldn't be alone at a time like this." Having served as both a chaplain and a parish pastor who had discussed mom's final moments with her, I asked who she wanted me to call. My sister and my husband quickly arrived, and mom didn't seize again. We covered her with a quilt that our son and his wife made and gifted her that Christmas as well as an afghan that her mother made. She no longer answered by shaking her head but instead squeezed our hands to respond.

After eight hours had passed, they admitted her to the hospital and took her to another room. Our son asked if he should hop on a plane, but the medical staff thought she would be gone before he arrived. "Wish I had just told him to come," I shared with my husband as the hours continued to pass. At around midnight, I suggested my husband go home and get some rest. He had already been there for 12 hours.

My sister and I remained, alternating between a cot and a chair that allowed us to hold mom's hands. When slumber disconnected us, it also awakened us to hold her hands again. As her breathing began to gurgle, I recalled all the bedside transitions I had midwifed and knew her last breaths were coming. Together, my sister and I spontaneously began to sing, "You are my Sunshine, My only Sunshine," one of our mother's favorite songs. Our grandfather sang it to our grandmother whenever he was holding a skein of yarn for her to wind into a ball for crocheting.

At 2:30 a.m., 16.5 hours after we had arrived, she took her last breath with no exhale as we sang this song. Shortly thereafter, a nurse arrived at the door to inform us mom had passed as the two of us continued to hold her hands. When my sister left, I remained—still talking to my mom and explaining everything that was happening. Some say the spirit lingers after it leaves the body, and I didn't want her to be alone. At the same time, I knew she was no longer there.

When I called to tell my husband that she had transitioned, he was at the door with electricians because the power box on the corner of our property blew a fuse at the same time my mom passed. The electricians reported the fire hazard that existed because of tree trimming the town needed to do. They assured him they would return at a saner hour the next day to do the trimming. I am convinced that my mom used the energy she acquired in passing to warn us of this danger. Synchronistic event by synchronistic event, she helps expand a portal.

After the fuse box and the moth visit there have been other mystical experiences. Since my mom died, if I can't find my keys, I ask her to help me find them. They are always in the very next place I look, even if I already looked there. Once, I drove to a neighborhood rummage in a subdivision I had never entered before. At the first stop, there were four placemats with gallery art on them: Vincent Van Gogh's Sunflowers, Paul Gauguin's Vision After the Sermon, Claude Monet's Waterlilies, and Mary Cassatt's The Child's Bath.

"What a coincidence, I saw all four of these pieces uncrated for exhibits at The Art Institute of Chicago when I consulted there," I said to the woman behind the table.

"Do you like art?" the homeowner asked. "Come inside and see what I did to the walls."

Following her into the house, I saw the Arizona mountainscape on the living room walls.

"Beautiful," I started saying, but then, suddenly, I felt as if an arm was around my waist, and another was slung over my shoulder by my neck. Tears flowed as I apologized to my host. "I am so sorry, but I feel like someone is hugging me around my waist and shoulders."

"Oh, that's Raphael. He came to bring your mother for a visit today," she replied without any hesitation. I had never met this woman, had not told her about my mother's death, and had to ask how she knew this.

"I am told," she said. "That's why I painted the mountains on my walls. All souls meet here. Now take a minute to enjoy your visit."

I closed my eyes and stood there smiling for I do not know how long. I couldn't help crying, but I felt so happy at the same time. When the hugging feeling stopped, I opened my eyes to find myself standing alone in the room. "Thank you," I called into the house.

"Love you," came the response that sounded like my mother as I opened the door to exit. What does one do with such a life-changing experience? It energized and inspired me to trust myself, turn inward, and take risks to follow what I found there. I no longer needed others to affirm what I discovered or to change others in order to live according to my intuition and resonance. The culmination of these mystical experiences freed me to walk within and find the love and wisdom mysteriously hidden there.

After this realization, I participated in a "Love, Letters, and Art" workshop at the Creativity and Expressive Therapies Summit in L.A. During the introduction, the facilitator suggested that one of the secrets kept in families that may be even greater than trauma is unstated love. My father left when I was 18 months old. He died of a heart attack when he was 47. I never had the chance to tell him I loved him because I didn't know him.

As the facilitator continued describing the class, I began to weep, realizing that I didn't register for it to create an anniversary gift for my husband, but to state my love for a father I never knew—in this world.

We began by listing 20 positive traits of the person who would receive our letters. How could I complete a list such as this for someone I didn't know? Then we wrote about our favorite memories—I only had one from when I was nine months old. I did also connect with him energetically through scrying. Finally, we wrote Haikus to inform the loving potential of our letters. These words drew me deeper within and I wrote the following letter:

Dear Dad:

I never got a chance to tell you "I Love You," because you left before I could. By the time I was an adult, much anger and resentment welled up inside of me from the abandonment and abuse experienced during your absence when mom married again. Our family was torn apart by all the arguing about sister's wedding and whether you or mom's second husband would walk her down the aisle. I distanced myself from the drama.

Then you died so young. I am sorry that my heart was not yet ready to receive you. But as it opened and scars healed, I learned more about you. I recall, discover, and realize your presence from beyond the grave.

I remember sitting in bed with you on what feels like a lazy Sunday morning—you reading the newspaper and me eating soda crackers from a sleeve on the bed. The memory makes me feel happy, I seem so content. Recently I found a newspaper article about you teaching women how to compete in Judo near the campus where I was doing my undergraduate work. This makes me wonder if you really wanted sons rather than daughters as I grew up hearing or if you possibly outgrew the preference.

I witnessed your focus and controlled movements while scrying. More of a memory than a vision, it felt like you took me with you to work. You held my hand as we walked through the door and you found me a seat. Then you started teaching. You looked so strong and powerful-like the international champion you are.

I am beginning to know your family as we research ancestry. Both of your parents died young, but your grandparents lived long lives. Did I ever meet them? I am interested to learn more about the free mason threads and the Native peoples living in the community in Canada where your family settled after immigrating from England. Did you know your family's history? Can't help wondering if our grandson's athletic abilities are somehow connected to you and if our granddaughter's persistence comes from you. It makes me smile to think so.

Thank you for your willingness to connect with me as my heart opens. I am sure that we share some understanding of everything being composed of energy and that our energies connect throughout matter, time, and place. I feel your presence as I meditate.

With a grateful heart that knows we are connected for you to hear...I love you, Dad!

After we finished writing, we created our art pieces. Selecting two oil pastels in different colors, we blindly placed lines on paper. Then we opened our eyes and colored in the lines. When I opened my eyes, the heart jumped out at me. I colored it red between the green and purple colors with which I selected to draw blindly. Next, we filled in the spaces. A hand holding the heart emerged along with a blue bodied silhouette. For me this image demonstrates and affirms the energetic connection that my father and I share through love.

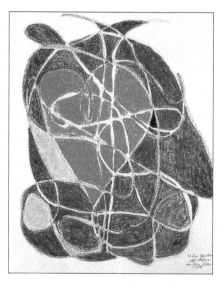

Crystal's blind drawing.

From beyond the grave my parents set aside their heartbreak to help expand a portal that allowed me to walk within myself not only to find my father's love for me, but to also help me find my love for him. This was so difficult for mom while she was alive that she cut his head out of every photo we owned. Their actions helped me consciously connect with both the

Divine Feminine energies of my intuition, creativity, and compassion, and the Sacred Masculine energies of inclusiveness, connectedness, and service. These attributes are not defined by gender, but by the nature of the spirit within each one of us.

Being wounded is part of being human. Astrologers today note this by including Chiron, technically a comet or a minor planet in readings. They reference Chiron in terms of wounded healing. The decision we make at each point of choice is whether we will live by festering lesions or healing scars. Choosing involves an ongoing process, just as healing does. None of us reaches a state of healing that no longer requires our conscious presence. Yet, we can heal enough to see beyond the wounds to find love within ourselves, within others and even within the most unexpected places.

Now, when I meditate with my palms facing up and relaxed on my knees, I sense my father's hand in my right, my mother's hand in my left, and I feel Whole. I know the circle is complete because they too are holding hands. Tears flow and I smile each time I feel this. For such Wholeness fosters compassion, love, and beauty even in the midst of chaos, suffering, and death.

FREE GIFT

My Gift to You:

A recorded Introduction to The Gospel of Mary one-hour class.

To access, visit **www.crystalsteinbergcocreating.com**

Inside lid and outside of keepsake box that Crystal designed
following her mother's transition.

Crystal L. Steinberg *synthesizes material and spiritual worlds, masculine and feminine energies, and ancient and future understandings to bring Wholeness forward in the chaos of birthing a new world. This Wholeness offers Compassion, Love and Beauty.*

As the creator of the Unlearning Religious Dogma Series, Crystal writes for anyone exploring their spiritual nature. Her first book in the series, Walk Within: Reclaim Your Spiritual Nature—An Advent, Christmas, & Solstice Path *is an Amazon bestseller.*

Sharing experiences from her personal journey, she co-creates safe space for vulnerable explorations that inspire readers to identify and share their resonances, agreements and how they acquire them. Crystal's artwork offers encouragement and support along the way.

Her MAT, MDiv, Certifications and Wisdom Studies PhD Candidate credentials demonstrate research scholarship, while her teaching, ordination, parish service, intuitive healing, initiations, and intentional co-creativity reveal her willingness to serve.

Crystal writes in her scriptorium, makes custom nesting dolls in her studio, and speaks and facilitates workshops virtually or locally in nature's magical lake environment of central Wisconsin.

Learn about all of her offerings at **crystalsteinbergcocreating.com**

CHAPTER 16

Becoming Spirit-Led

How a Health Crisis Transformed My Life

By Dr. Heather Kristian Strang

This was hardly a time for respectable clothing. Instead, I sat mid-day at my two-top dining table dressed in ragged pajamas—an oversized t-shirt and old workout leggings re-purposed from the days when I would wake every morning and head directly to the gym. Now the thought of such a task exhausted me. Besides, I had a much bigger task before me. I had been diagnosed with a cystic tumor the size of a grapefruit attached to one of my ovaries, and the doctors had performed emergency surgery to remove it. "It's just like fixing a flat tire," the grey-haired surgeon assured me. He of course thought this metaphor would calm me. It didn't.

In fact, what infuriated me the most about this situation was that I was an overall healthy human. At 29, I worked out regularly, ate gluten-dairy-soy-refined-sugar-free, had a group of friends, was in a good relationship with a nice guy (bet you know how it turned out by that description, eh?), and lived in a beautiful condo in the trees, amidst some of Portland, Oregon's finest nature. I was living my life's dream as a writer—a freelance writer, so not the full breadth of my dream, but close enough anyway. I had great editors and I had even started doing some web TV dining reviews, including covering International Food Day for the local news affiliate. Things were looking up for me.

But then, seemingly out of nowhere, the pain, the diagnosis, and the surgery. What was even more perplexing is that unlike the "flat tire" quick fix the surgeon assured me this would be—the surgery catapulted me into greater states of pain, inflammation, anxiety, and bleeding, as well as rapid weight loss despite eating consistently. So, while I was allegedly tumor-free I became sicker than I had been prior to the surgery. Obviously, all-day-long pajamas were the only thing that would do for times like these.

I also had my trusty journal by my side. My journal had gotten me through almost every tragedy—starting at 15 when I was immersed in a painful life with an abusive mother, absent father, and new horrific stepfather. My writing was my saving grace. And so of course, I had my journal right with me for this devastating time, paired with a deck of Fairy Oracle cards. Yep, you read that right, I said Fairy Oracle cards.

It was unusual behavior for me, but this time in my life practically required such extreme measures.

Though I was raised as a Jehovah's Witness (JW), I abandoned my religion of origin at age 24 and set forth to innerstand spirituality far and wide. I studied Buddhism, Kabbalah and Ba'hai, read up on Muslim and Hindu religions, and attended non-denominational Christian churches with rockstar bands (which was both surprising and confusing). I arrived at the same conclusion every single time—none of them were that dissimilar from the oppressive religion I had been raised in. They were simply dressed up to look a little different—that was all. With this discovery, I gave up on God.

I stopped praying, I stopped searching and I assumed the title of agnostic. I knew there had to be something more; I had felt it in brief moments while singing religious songs with tens of thousands at JW conventions. I had felt it sitting in my bathtub, surrounded by candles reading the Bible without any man or organization there to tell me what it all meant (the Song of Solomon, Psalms, and Proverbs were my favorite chapters).

But now, a diagnosis, surgery, and "recovery" that was feeling more like the start of a new illness—all in an otherwise healthy life—upended me. It not only wasn't fair or right, but I also had no one to blame, which is extraordinarily aggravating when one is in a deep state of victim consciousness like I was. I couldn't blame God as I had kicked Her out of my life at that point, I certainly couldn't blame myself (I mean, pllleeeaaasseee it's not like I created my reality or anything), I couldn't even blame the doctors. They were nice enough and had done their "job" by removing the tumor. So it was hopeless—there was literally no one to blame and nothing I could do.

Which is how I ended up with a Fairy Oracle deck.

When you're desperate and out of options, a Fairy Oracle deck doesn't seem too far out there anymore. I sat there shuffling the Oracle cards, unsure if I even believed in such divination methods. But then, thoughtlessly and seemingly out of nowhere I said out loud, "I'm done! I am done living from my mind. I want to be Spirit-Led!"

I didn't know what Spirit-Led meant, I had never heard that term before. Shouldn't I have said "heart-centered" or used some other self-development, psycho-babble term since I had spent 10 years in traditional talk therapy? Nope. I said Spirit-Led. Out of my head and into Spirit? What was Spirit and how was it going to lead me? And for crying out loud, where was it going to lead me to?

The only thing I knew about Spirit at that point was this: My high school friend had been brutally murdered three years previously and I was shaken. It brought up a lot of fear because since leaving the JWs and becoming "agnostic," I had no clue what I believed about death—or anything for that matter.

Then, unexpectedly, about a week after her "death," In the early morning hours I entered what I later learned was a lucid dream state. In it, my friend came to me. Her name is Dion (Hi, Dion—Love ya girl!). In this dream, we walked along the train tracks by our high school in our hometown on the Oregon Coast. As we walked, I confessed to her that I was afraid of her death. I had left my religion; I didn't know what my true beliefs were and now she had been murdered. How was I to make sense of that?

She explained to me in the most easeful of ways that she was just fine. She explained to me that death is not what we're told it is and that she had an agreement with the man who had killed her and what I now innerstand to be karma with him—and yet they still hadn't been able to bring things to a peaceful end. She shrugged her shoulders. No worries, she would return at some point and try her hand at it again.

I was so shocked and yet comforted by this exchange that I filed it away as something I would someday explore. I felt peace around her death and loved the moments when I thought I saw her in a crowd and when she would visit me in the dream state.

However, now I felt as though I was potentially facing my own death, and my previous comfort from Dion's dream messages was fading. I had lost faith in Western medicine, I had tried naturopathic care and some other "alternative" treatments, but nothing changed.

I closed my eyes, pulled a Fairy Oracle card, and hoped for the best.

"Mediumship."

See, I knew these damn cards didn't work. I re-shuffled the deck and tried again.

"Mediumship."

And again.

"Mediumship."

I slammed the cards down onto the table, convinced all was hopeless. Why in the f*** was I pulling a card that indicated I was to work as a medium and/or have a session with a medium and/or I had a special connection to non-physical energy, aka dead people?

I. Could. Not. Even.

I hopelessly lamented that even Fairy Oracle cards did not work for me. So, there was clearly only one option left for me now, and that was to figure out what in the heck living Spirit-Led meant.

A couple of weeks later I was attending an Understanding Men seminar by Alison Armstrong. I was in a stable relationship with a nice man, and yet…there had to be something more than that…wasn't there? I thought perhaps the workshop would help me uncover what that was.

Instead, I found myself talking to the woman sitting next to me, sharing about my diagnosis, surgery, and continued womb struggles. She began to speak about Brazil and spiritual healers there, as well as psychic surgeries. I had never been to Brazil nor desired to visit there, but as soon as she began speaking about it, I knew I had to go. She offered for me to go with her as she had a trip planned in the fall of the next year, and she had been playing with the idea of working as a guide to Brazil for these healings.

At this point, I had never had a psychic anything and I didn't have any idea what I was getting into. But it mattered not; I had to go. The following night, I dreamed of Brazil, of being on the land, and of the psychic surgery. I booked my trip shortly after.

My boyfriend, who also described himself as agnostic, was pretty sure I was losing it. Oracle cards, talk of being Spirit-Led, and now a Brazil trip he knew I couldn't afford with a woman I had just met—all qualified me in his eyes as living precariously close to crazy-town. Not surprisingly, he wasn't going with me.

I struggled for some time about ending that relationship—I mean, what girl wouldn't have been happy with it? He was committed, loyal, stable, kind, funny, and wanted to be with me. As long as I stayed, you know, the way he wanted me to be—an agnostic writer who went to costume parties with him, drank lots of wine, had a regular group of familiar friends, jogged on the weekends, and did all the things that someone does when they're living the program of how to do life in the Western world in their 20s and 30s.

There was more, I was sure of it. I had no proof, but something within me kept repeating over and over again, Spirit-Led, Spirit-led. I had to find out how to live Spirit-Led because my programmed life was not going to cut it for me any longer. My freelance writing wasn't going to, either. I knew I needed to serve, as I suddenly had this insatiable desire to help others and be of benefit to them.

It was 2008 and coaching was becoming a whole thing. My best friend at the time was a coach and loved it. Turns out all I needed was my bachelor's degree for this; I didn't need a master's degree back then—so that meant I could train as a coach and be of service immediately.

Synchronistically, I was led to a job listing for a coaching company that would train me, pay me, and provide me with hundreds of clients to coach. I was in. But before I could agree to take the job, I let them know I had a two-week sojourn to Brazil planned that fall and could not miss it. They honored my request, and I dove into the training and assisting others.

I was skinny as f***, so much so that before I left for Brazil, my little sister pulled me aside to let me know I had a bobble-head situation happening—meaning my body was so emaciated my head looked like, well you get it—

a bobble-head. I honestly hadn't noticed; I was so lit up by coaching others, I had moved into a studio apartment in trendy NW Portland, and I was sure that the psychic surgery in Brazil was going to be the key to my healing.

I received emails from that "nice" ex-boyfriend before the surgery, condescendingly saying he "hoped I got what I was looking for." All the while reiterating that he thought the "spiritual journey" I was on was nuts. What a nice guy, huh? Perhaps my intuition had known better. My family didn't get it either, which was no surprise, seeing as I was the cliché black sheep of the family, exploring territory they thought was pure bananas.

Visiting Brazil was like returning to a land that I had known long ago. The smells, the food (tapioca cheese bread, anyone?), the people, the language—I was remembering it from another time. I was enlivened.

However, on the morning of the psychic surgery, I became incredibly afraid. Like, in tears, what-in-the-actual-fuck-am-I-doing afraid. A kind man from New Zealand took me aside to comfort me and remind me that I was protected and supported. I wasn't sure who exactly I was protected by, but his words did make me feel better. I felt alone and frightened. Even so, that did not deter me. I had flown halfway across the world, so I was going to have to put on my big girl panties and do the damn thing.

And so, into a room of 30 or more people I went. A woman I did not know or speak to privately or beforehand instructed us to close our eyes. She told us to place our hands on whatever part of our body wanted to be healed. I instinctively placed one hand on my heart and one hand on my womb. Then, she said an anesthetic was being placed in those areas so we would not feel the pain of the surgery. A slight smile formed at my mouth. They were really trying to make this seem authentic, weren't they? My fear was now being replaced by skepticism. Even so, I did as I was instructed and then the woman began to pray over us in Portuguese.

Suddenly, I, along with everyone else in the room, began to wail and sob and cry. Inside my body, things were MOVING. There was a knocking in my knee, a knocking in my womb, a knocking in my heart—from the inside OUT. As quickly as I and everyone in the room had started crying and screaming (the woman behind me was literally banging into the back of my chair from the ferocity of her wailing), it stopped.

I felt at peace. The "surgery" was over. What had seemed like a few mere minutes had been almost 30 and I was instructed to go to my pousada room and not leave my bed for 24 hours, as I'd had surgery. This felt comical to me, but I was so dazed from the "surgery" experience that I agreed. For hours I lay in my room on a twin bed, staring at the ceiling. My mind buzzed at a million miles an hour.

I devoured the lunch brought to me and wondered if I would notice anything different from this whole experience. Two hours later, I awoke from a deep sleep and could not move my body. All of my life force energy was gone, and my womb was on fire—it felt as though knives had been slicing around inside of me. I was terrified. I was so terrified that I did something I had not done in years.

I began to pray. I began to pray and beg and plead with a God I had ignored for many years to save my life. I prayed, insisting that if I was allowed to live, I would devote my entire life to The Divine. I would do as The Divine wanted for me in this lifetime.

Suddenly I heard laughter. Some of the other women staying at the pousada had miraculously gathered around the entrance of my room, talking and laughing, bringing a high vibration of joy that immediately soothed me. My anxiety eased. I was going to be okay.

On some nights in Brazil, I would wake up to golden orbs of light hovering over my body. Rather than feeling afraid I would feel their tremendous Love and fall back into a deep sleep. It took roughly four days for me to be able to walk again, but by the time the two weeks were up, I had gained all my weight back (thank you cheese bread, peanut butter bars and amazing home-cooked Brazilian food) and looked like a completely new woman. The inflammation in my womb was gone and so was the incessant bleeding, anxiety, and insomnia. In its place was warm energy coming from the palms of my hands and a sudden "knowing" about things I should not have known about.

From that moment on, my life was never the same. My coaching clients went to new levels of success, I won awards from the coaching company I worked for, I moved to Kauai (in three weeks' time), and I started to explore healing modalities with which I could use the healing energy coming from my hands.

I lost a lot of "friends" and romantic partners and called in new, more aligned ones. I found joy in being of service and assisting others in living their Highest Path. I got over my fear of "dead" people and ended up doing exactly what that Fairy Oracle had predicted all along—I was a medium as it turned out (and don't even get me started about what I had to do with that line of "dead people" in my room when I was shown that gift).

Today I work as an author and metaphysical psychologist assisting those Souls called to me in living their Highest Destiny and in co-creating their own sovereign and prosperous heaven-on-Earth, Golden Age. My 29-year-old self, sitting at that dining table in ratty old pajamas would never have believed that I would end up here, but what an amazing Spirit-led Adventure it has been. It has changed everything for the better and I wouldn't change it for the world.

FREE GIFT

My Gift to You:

A free Sacred Love transmission from Mary Magdalene through Dr. Kristian

To access, visit **www.Sacred-Spirituality.org**

DR. HEATHER KRISTIAN STRANG *is a metaphysical psychologist and an Amazon bestselling author. She's written ten books in the genres of visionary fiction, paranormal romance, and channeled message Oracles. Basically, everything she Loves, she writes about! Kristian has been featured in publications such as Bustle, The Huffington Post, Elephant Journal, Thrive Global, Elite Daily and on the cover of the Sedona Journal of Emergence. She's also been a featured speaker on a number of podcasts and summits, including her own, "Awakening: The Podcast."*

Dr. Strang is currently finishing her eleventh book, Love Letters from Mary Magdalene: The Untold Tale of her Life, Love & Legacy. *When she's not doing all of that, you'll find her dance-walking on the Oregon Coast or baking it up in the kitchen for her intuitive eating blog, Metaphysical Menu.*

Learn more: **www.Sacred-Spirituality.org**

More Books by Flower of Life Press

  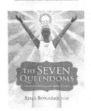  

Made in USA - Kendallville, IN
83270_9798987395400
12.13.2022 1352